Handle that new call with care:

Accepting or declining a call to a new congregation

David Campbell

©Day One Publications 2009
First printed 2009

A CIP record is held at the British Library

ISBN 978-1-84625-153-5

Published by Day One Publications, Ryelands Road, Leominster, HR6 8NZ
☎ 01568 613 740
FAX 01568 611 473
email—sales@dayone.co.uk
web site—www.dayone.co.uk
North American e-mail—usasales@dayone.co.uk
North American web site—www.dayonebookstore.com

Cover designed by Wayne McMaster
Printed by Orchard Press Cheltenham Ltd.

ENDORSEMENTS

In this little book, David Campbell has dealt with a theme that is among the most important in any minister's life, yet among the least tackled in pastoral literature: what is a minister to do when a church calls him away from the congregation in which he is currently ministering? By looking at ministerial biographies, David has gleaned important principles and suggestions to guide a minister in this most crucial of all dilemmas. By drawing on his own experience and that of others, he has written a book which will be of immense value in helping ministers recognize God's leading in their lives.

Revd Dr Iain D. Campbell
Free Church of Scotland, Isle of Lewis, UK

Biblical principles joined to wise counsel and illustrated from Christian biography are the nuts and bolts of this much-needed book. Those who seek ironclad formulas for resolving vexing questions of guidance will be disappointed. Those who are looking for balanced perspectives on the issues addressed will be thankful to David Campbell for his labours. The author has mined deeply and extensively in the field of Christian biography. In doing so, he has unearthed rich treasures of godly wisdom, telling illustrations and helpful cautions for any who are wrestling with the question, 'Shall I accept a call to another sphere of ministerial labour?' I trust the book will be widely read and its wisdom heeded.

Albert N. Martin
Former pastor of Trinity Baptist Church, Montville, New Jersey, USA

Pastor Campbell has made a significant contribution for us all with this fine book. The entire area of a pastor considering whether he should accept a call to another pastoral charge, thereby leaving his own flock, is a complex matter which contains a veritable mass of issues and can be one of the most difficult experiences through which a man and his church can go. This work examines a host of considerations without giving simplistic guidance. There are questions for the man to face on a number of levels—his own spiritual livelihood, his gifts, his experience, his family, the church he is leaving, and, of course, the church to which he would consider moving. David Campbell's treatment will be a great blessing to men and churches facing this complicated and emotional time in their lives.

Revd Robert B. Selph
Senior Pastor, Grace Baptist Church, Taylors, South Carolina, USA

At many points I saw myself in David Campbell's book. The quotations from pastors who left a much-loved congregation were especially touching. But I expect that the greatest value of this book will be for those who are contemplating a move. The advice is theologically solid and salted with the wisdom of experience. I believe every pastor should read this book and then keep it for the day he may need it. I also commend this book to church members as it may help them to understand why pastors sometimes move from one church to another.

Revd Gordon Taylor
Co-ordinator, Association of Reformed Baptist Churches of America

Dedication
To Megan and Caitriona

ACKNOWLEDGEMENTS

The following friends and colleagues took time to read through the manuscript: Iain D. Campbell, Walter Chantry, Scott Leone, Albert N. Martin, Mike McKelvey, Tom Richwine, Bob Selph and Gordon Taylor. My wife, Mairi, very kindly went over it as well. I greatly appreciate their willingness to do this and their helpful suggestions. Special thanks are due to Iain D. Campbell, Albert N. Martin, Bob Selph and Gordon Taylor for their warm commendations of the book.

CONTENTS

Introduction

judgement, a more important function than to fill one pulpit or superintend one parish anywhere'.[5]

Other examples of 'Ministers not in Pastoral Office' (to borrow one of Harvey's chapter headings[6]) include the evangelist who moves from place to place; the Bible teacher who does the same; the home or foreign missionary who is beginning an entirely new gospel work; the representative of a denomination or association of churches set apart for a wider work of ministry among the constituent congregations and the missionaries they support. Then there is the retired pastor. By virtue of his retirement he has ceased to be a pastor. But if he continues to have the requisite gifts for ministering God's Word, the moral qualities that fit him for such a ministry, the desire for it, and opportunities for its exercise, he is warranted in concluding that the call of God upon his life to be a minister of God's Word remains.

The concern of this book, however, is not with 'Ministers *not* in Pastoral Office', but rather with those who are. For the furtherance of his gracious purposes towards sinners the Lord, in innumerable instances, has called men to be ministers of his Word within the context of a pastorate. Their preaching and teaching ministry is primarily directed to a specific congregation and to the community in which it is placed. They rightly think of themselves, and are viewed by the congregations they serve, as *pastors*. But their most basic calling is to be ministers of the Word of the Lord. It is what they are before they enter into a pastoral charge; it is what they are as they fulfil its duties; it is what they continue to be when they leave the pastorate. They are first and foremost servants of God's Word. They have, however, a *specific* calling to minister that Word to a particular congregation for a particular period of time as its pastor.

The question of the call

How is this call to a pastoral ministry to be discerned? Since it is a question on which much has been written, and since this book is for those who are already in pastoral ministry rather than for those who are thinking about entering it, the temptation is to skip the question altogether and move on! A word or two, however, may be helpful.

The most obvious starting point is the qualifications for the pastoral office outlined in passages like 1 Timothy 3 and Titus 1. No one who lacks these qualifications ought to think that God—at least at that particular time in his life—is calling him to be a pastor of a congregation. A prospective candidate needs to examine himself carefully in the light of these Scriptures—as does the congregation that is thinking of having him as one of its overseers. He must, for example, have the requisite teaching gifts (1 Tim. 3:2). In addition, 'He must hold firmly to the trustworthy message as it has been taught, so that he can encourage others by sound doctrine and refute those who oppose it' (Titus 1:9). And then there are all the personal qualities that he must display. In both of the above letters, Paul insists that a prospective pastor must be a certain kind of husband, a certain kind of father, and a certain kind of Christian man in general.

Normally there will be, in addition to a fitness for the task, a desire for it, too. The Timothy passage begins with the assumption that Christian men will set their hearts on being overseers, and it is usually the case that when God himself is calling a man to that office, a God-given desire for it will be there. That will especially be the case with the man who is being called to devote himself *wholly* to pastoral work and to make preaching, teaching and pastoral care his life's work. There have been some notable exceptions. The two great 16th-century Reformers, John Knox and John Calvin, for example, both initially shrank from the responsibilities of pastoral ministry. Normally, however, when God has his hand upon a man for this himself and his biblical predecessors. We limit ourselves, by way of illustration, to a small selection bearing on the subject of this book. We will return to some of them later.

When the Revd Hugh Heugh, minister of the United Secession church in Stirling, Scotland, was called in 1821 to a church in Glasgow, he subjected himself to 'a serious process of examination and inquiry'. His first question for consideration was: *'Is translation* [i.e. to another congregation] *scriptural?'*[9] A few years earlier, Thomas Chalmers, at that time minister of the Church of Scotland in Kilmany, in anticipation of a call also to Glasgow, set down on a sheet of paper in parallel columns the arguments for leaving and staying. His first reason for staying in Kilmany was simply that it was his 'present situation'. He then added these words: 'but moving from place to place was the general practice of the first preachers'.[10] That is apparent both in Acts and in the apostolic letters. Ministers of the Word like Paul, Barnabas, Titus and Timothy did have settled ministries in particular places, but only for a period of time, shorter or longer, and then they moved on somewhere else. We infer from that—in answer to Heugh's question— that translation to another congregation *is* scriptural. For the furtherance of his kingdom, the Lord is at liberty to call his servants to minister in another place, just as he did in the church's early days.

'But who will take my place?' If a minister *is* to leave his congregation, one of his primary concerns, if he has a truly pastoral heart, will be with this question of a successor. This was Moses' concern as he drew near to the end of his time as leader of Israel: 'Moses said to the LORD, "May the LORD, the God of the spirits of all mankind, appoint a man over this community to go out and come in before them, one who will lead them out and bring them in, so that the LORD's people will not be like sheep without a shepherd"' (Num. 27:15–17). His sense of the deprivation the people were about to suffer and

of the need that there was for someone to take his place drove him to prayer. And in the answer God gave to Moses, what an encouragement for the minister today to pray likewise! 'Take Joshua son of Nun ... At his command he and the entire community of the Israelites will go out and at his command they will come in' (Num. 27:18, 21).

What will cause a minister to remain where he is? Perhaps what kept Titus in Crete. He stayed on there after the apostle Paul left in order to 'straighten out what was left unfinished' (Titus 1:5). There were things that still needed to be done (such as the appointment of elders), situations that needed to be tackled (particularly the problem of false teachers) and truths that needed to be taught (both to the church as a whole and to particular groups), and until these things were done it was Titus's duty to stay where he was. So it is with many a minister today.

Should a minister leave *because he's facing difficulties?* It is often the Lord's will that he continue his ministry in spite of them. How helpful, in so many such cases, is the prophet Jeremiah. We know what difficulties he faced—widespread resistance to the truth, enemies who were out to get him, very little fruit to show for his years of hard work. And there were times when he wanted out! But the Lord had assigned him his post and by his grace he stuck to it. We have in him the most steadying, encouraging, humbling and inspiring of examples— one that has helped many a sorely tried minister to submit to the Lord's will and stay where he is.

Or, to take a final example, is there *uncertainty* about the decision? In some way or other the Lord will certainly guide us. We may have to wait for some considerable time, as Paul and his companions did before it was clear that they were to go to Macedonia (Acts 16). But as surely as light arose for those ministers, it will arise for us as well.

Who's asking the question?

We return, then, to the chapter title, and to the question which it is not self-evident that a pastor under call to a congregation might begin by asking: 'What *am* I?' He is first and foremost a minister of the Word of God. The decision that he is wrestling with, to state it accurately, is, 'Should I, *a minister of the Word*, who for ____ years has been serving as pastor of _____ accept a call to _____?' Putting it in that way does not, of course, answer his question. But it points him in the direction of the ample biblical materials that, in connection with his biblical predecessors, the Lord has provided for his guidance.

Who is ultimately to decide?

The Lord Jesus is the Chief Shepherd, and it is his mind alone that we must seek.

–Derek Prime

The calling church has extended its call. The pastor who has received it must eventually give his answer. But who is *ultimately* to decide? The answer springs immediately to our lips. As servants of Jesus Christ, ministering his Word in accordance with his will, we recognize that the final decision lies with him. He is sovereign over his church—over its members and its ministers—and therefore it is his will on the matter that must prevail.

Authority

Scripture uses a number of images to give expression to this sovereignty. One is the image of the *head*. The church is frequently portrayed as a body of which Christ is the head. In Ephesians 4, for example, Paul speaks of 'the body of Christ' growing up 'into him who is the Head, that is, Christ', and then adds that 'From him the whole body, joined and held together by every supporting ligament, grows and builds itself up in love, as each part does its work' (vv. 12, 15–16). In the following chapter he returns to the image in connection with the subject of marriage: 'Wives, submit to your husbands as to the Lord. For the husband is the head of the wife as Christ is the head of the church, his body' (5:22–23). It is clear from this latter reference that headship involves authority. Christ is certainly the church's *loving* head, and husbands, in the exercise of their own headship, are to model Christ's amazing love. But he is also the church's *authoritative* head, and recognizing that, 'the church submits to Christ' (5:24), endeavouring in its doctrine, worship and practice to implement his revealed will.

A second image is that of the *shepherd*. We rightly associate this with costly, self-sacrificing love. Christ is 'the good shepherd' who 'lays down his life for the sheep' (John 10:11). But the shepherd is also an authority figure. The sheep hear his voice and follow him (John 10:3–4). He makes them to lie down in green pastures and leads them beside quiet waters (Ps. 23:2). In passages like Ezekiel 34 the image of shepherd is used of the kings of Israel. And in the New Testament Christ is spoken of as 'the Chief Shepherd' who entrusts men with his flock and promises them a crown of glory if they fulfil their duties faithfully (1 Peter 5:2–5).

And then there is the *overseer*. 'For you were like sheep going astray,' says Peter in his first letter, 'but now you have returned to the Shepherd and Overseer of your souls' (2:25). The reference is to Jesus. Interestingly, in Acts 20, Paul brings together the same concepts of shepherding and overseeing in his address to the Ephesian elders. He says to them, 'Keep watch over yourselves and all the flock of which the Holy Spirit has made you overseers. Be shepherds of the church of God' (v. 28). A pastor is an overseer. The Spirit has given him pastoral oversight of a congregation. His duty is to watch over it and take care of it; to protect it and to promote its spiritual well-being. He does so, however, as an instrument in the hand of the Lord Jesus and under his authority. As the Shepherd and Overseer of our souls, it is he who has the *supreme* oversight, both of the congregation as a whole and of the individual members who make it up.

Gifts to the church

One of the things that Jesus does in the exercise of his sovereignty is to give ministers of the Word to his church. In the classic text on the subject Paul tells us that 'It was he'— the ascended Lord—'who gave some to be apostles, some to be prophets, some to be evangelists, and some to be pastors and teachers.' These men are his gifts to the church, given in order 'to prepare God's people for works of service, so that

26

the body of Christ may be built up until we all reach unity
in the faith and in the knowledge of the Son of God and
become mature, attaining to the whole measure of the fulness
of Christ' (Eph. 4:11–13). Of especial interest here is his gift
of pastors. In answer to his people's prayers and in response
to his church's needs he saves, equips and prepares men for
pastoral ministry, inwardly calls them to the work, and leads
particular congregations to set them apart for that work.

Then there is the statement of Paul in Acts 20 quoted above.
Certain men had pastoral oversight of the Ephesian church
because the Holy Spirit had *made* them overseers (v. 28). As
the agent of the ascended Christ, the Spirit had been at work—
granting these men new birth, endowing them with the requisite
spiritual gifts for the task of oversight, working in them those
qualities of Christian character that were just as necessary
as their abilities, enabling the congregation to discern their
fitness, and inclining their hearts to accept the invitation to be
'shepherds of the church of God' (v. 28).

We note a similar divine activity in connection with the
ministers of the Old Testament church. We saw in the previous
chapter that one of the duties of the priests was to teach the
law of God (Mal. 2:7; Deut. 33:8, 10). For this priestly work it
was the Lord himself who chose the tribe of Levi. So, too, the
prophets for their special ministry. A true prophet prophesied to
the people because of the call of God on his life and because God
gave him a message to deliver.

It is evident, then, *throughout* biblical history that in God's
people having ministers, a divine hand is to be discerned. The
Lord knows that one of our great and unchanging needs is for
men to bring to us his Word. And through the appointing of Old
Testament prophets and priests, and New Testament apostles,
prophets, evangelists, pastors and teachers, that need both has
been and continues to be supplied.

Moving them on

The same sovereignty that appoints, however, also moves ministers on. We have a striking example of this in Acts 13. 'In the church at Antioch there were prophets and teachers: Barnabas, Simeon called Niger, Lucius of Cyrene, Manaen … and Saul. While they were worshipping the Lord and fasting, the Holy Spirit said, "Set apart for me Barnabas and Saul for the work to which I have called them"' (vv. 1–2). For a time Saul and Barnabas had been ministering God's Word in the Antioch church, but it was now the Lord's will that they move on to a new work. Accordingly, we read that 'after they had fasted and prayed, they placed their hands on them and sent them off' (v. 3).

We see similar manifestations of divine sovereignty elsewhere in the book of Acts. An angel of the Lord calls Philip away from Samaria to preach to the Ethiopian eunuch. Peter is summoned from Joppa to Caesarea by a vision and a voice from heaven. Paul is constantly being moved on from place to place by a providence at work through persecution. In the events that take the same apostle to Macedonia (Acts 16), we have the Holy Spirit keeping him from preaching in one place, the Spirit of Jesus not permitting him to enter another place, and at last a vision of a man from Macedonia pleading with him to come over and help them.

In most of these examples reference is explicitly made to a divine hand at work. What about the many other instances where no such reference is to be found? May we assume the same divine leading? There is the highest likelihood that we may. Certainly, there is not a hint of the Lord's disapproval. Quite the reverse. When we read in Acts 11, for example, of Barnabas bringing Saul to Antioch from Tarsus (where presumably he had been ministering God's Word), or in Acts 16 of Paul taking Timothy from Lystra (where his good reputation had probably as much to do with his usefulness as a preacher as his personal character), we are evidently intended to discern the Lord's hand at work, advancing his kingdom by means of these changes. The Lord's ministers in New Testament days were at the beck and call of their heavenly Master, ministering the Word in a particular place for a certain period of time, longer or shorter, and then, according to his sovereign determination, made known to them in a variety of ways, moving on to somewhere else.

Crown rights

Dare anyone dispute the Lord's rights in this regard? He is King over his own kingdom, the Chief Shepherd of his own flock, the Head of his own body, the Overseer of all our souls. He has an incontestable liberty to consult the highest interests of his church and, as seems best to him, to move ministers of the gospel from one place to another or to keep them where they are.

Our specific concern, however, is with those gospel ministers whom he has placed in positions of pastoral responsibility. Does the Lord have the right to move these men from one congregation to another? To ask is to answer. We can see him exercising the right of removal in other ways. He takes some men from the pastoral office through the onset of ill health. Others he removes by death. Still others he permits to be forced from the pastorate through the persecuting activities of the enemies of the gospel. The reasons for such actions are always varied and often, to some degree, a mystery. But the reality of them cannot be disputed. In the exercise of his sovereign good pleasure the Lord in these ways brings pastorates to an end. May he not also bring them to an end by calling his servants to minister his Word to another congregation? We cannot confess Christ's supreme authority over his church and answer in the negative.

That he actually does so call is confirmed by the experience of tens of thousands of ministers over the centuries. After a period of time in one congregation they are invited to minister to another. They consider the matter prayerfully. They look to the Head of the church for wisdom to know if it is he who is moving them on. They come eventually to the conclusion that he is and take the step. And though there may be great sorrow at the parting and many difficulties to face in the new situation, they are strengthened by the inner conviction that their move has been undertaken at the bidding of the Lord himself. Are they mistaken? Some doubtless are. But is it conceivable that they *all* are? Other churches have needed pastors. They have prayed for them. They have looked to the exalted Christ to give them. And he has heard their prayers. In the exercise of his sovereignty over his church and in harmony with his New Testament manner of working he has taken men who are already ministers of the gospel and has moved them from one sphere of ministry to another.

As with the other ways in which he takes men from the pastorate, the Lord's reasons for moving them on are always varied and often, to some degree, a mystery. We will touch on some of them later in the book. Some relate to the *pastor himself*. The Lord considers his health, perhaps, or the opportunity that he will have to develop his gifts and usefulness, or the fact that he has suffered so much at the hands of hostile church members, or the level of maturity that he has reached that peculiarly fits him for the challenges of a new situation. And some, of course, relate to the *congregation that he is leaving*. The impact of the closing weeks of the old ministry; the challenges to faith as the people look to the Lord for the supply of their future pastoral needs; the chastisement of those who are justly deprived of a ministry that they have sinfully undervalued; the opportunity for the development of latent gifts in the congregation; or the rich benefits of the new ministry that the Lord has planned for them; the Lord considers all these and more in the decision that he takes to translate one of his servants to another congregation.

The length of a pastorate

We recognize, too, that the sovereignty that brings a pastorate to an end by transferring a man to another congregation has, in so doing, determined the length of that pastorate. There is much to be said for *long* pastorates. The opportunities that they give for developing deep relationships with the people, the growing influence for good that a pastor can have as those relationships develop, the healthy discipline of continually having to break fresh ground in preaching, the long-term goals that can be striven for, the enrichment to the congregation as the pastor matures over the years in gifts and graces; these are all arguments for a pastor putting down roots and remaining in a charge for a considerable length of time.

Furthermore, for these and other reasons, the Head of the church has often ordained that his servants remain *long* in a church, perhaps for the entirety of their pastoral ministry. The history of the church, from ancient times to the present, provides an abundance of examples. Names spring readily to mind. These men have had long pastorates and in the course of them (and, indeed, because of them) have done sterling work.

Nevertheless, for his own wise reasons, the Lord may move his servants on after very *short* pastorates. It is in keeping with what is to be observed of his ways in both Old and New Testaments. There is great variety in the length of time that he has had his servants minister his Word in particular places. The apostle Paul, for example, stayed weeks with some congregations, years with others. It is admittedly an area in which men may err, moving on after relatively short ministries when they ought to stay put. But it is also an area in which the Lord exercises his rightful sovereignty, moving his servants from one sphere to another when, to human judgement, a longer ministry might well have seemed preferable.

Submission

The one thing that remains for consideration in this chapter is the attitude that should be maintained towards the Lord as his will in the matter is considered. How should congregations and ministers respond when the Lord's will is made known? What should be their posture as they wait for it to be disclosed? One word sums it up better than any other. Throughout the whole process, the attitude of all concerned should be one of *submission*: the Lord's will be done.

A lovely example of what submission looks like in practice is to be seen in the following 'expression of ... continued attachment', recorded by the congregation of the Free High Church in Kilmarnock, Scotland, when their minister, the Revd Thomas Main, to their deep regret, accepted a call in 1857 to a church in Edinburgh:

> The union that has so long subsisted between him
> and his flock having been one of unbroken harmony
> and love, they fondly hope that though the tender
> tie which bound them together as pastor and people
> be dissolved, the same affectionate feeling and
> sympathy for each other may continue to exist. Their
> prayer is, that the blessing of the great head of the
> Church may rest abundantly on him in that portion
> of the vineyard to which he goes, and that the Spirit's
> influence may ever accompany his labours, both
> in public and private, making him instrumental in
> drawing many sinners to Jesus, and in building up
> and comforting His people in their most holy faith.[1]

This submission on the part of a congregation is to have its counterpart in the submission of its minister—either to stay where he is or to leave. In 1930, after eleven years as minister of a Free Church of Scotland congregation on the Isle of Skye, the Revd Kenneth MacRae found himself asking, 'Why am I kept here?' but then added, 'Let me wait patiently upon the Lord.'[2] A century earlier, Hugh Heugh of Stirling gave expression to the same submissiveness: 'I could remain here, or go any where, if only I could distinctly hear the voice of His authority bidding me.' And again, 'If I know myself, I have no other wish than this—to know the will of Him whom I desire to serve, and to whom, ere long, I must give an account.'[3] A third example, from an earlier century still, is the Revd Thomas Boston. When called from the Church of Scotland in Simprin to the Scottish Borders parish of Ettrick we read that, 'leaving all in God's hands, he was willing from the first to go or stay as the Lord might give the word'.[4] For a final example we cross the Atlantic. When Dr J. H. Thornwell was called to leave the South Carolina College in 1845 for a church in Baltimore, Maryland, he wrote to his friend Dr Breckinridge as follows: 'Had it been in my power to choose my own field of labour, I should never have thought of leaving South Carolina; but I bow to the will of a sovereign God, and acquiesce, without a murmur, in the plain intimations of his providence.'[5]

In the light of our Saviour's Lordship, there can be no better attitude than that.

Uncertainty

Chapter 3

What would I not give for a voice from heaven, to tell me what to do?

–Matthew Dickie

'I acknowledge that the Lord is sovereign in this matter,' says the pastor, 'and that he may move me on or keep me where I am as it pleases him. But how do I know what his will *is*?' In Chapters 4 and 5 we will look at a number of things that may helpfully be considered as we wrestle with that question. In this chapter, we focus on the fact that men are frequently *uncertain* what to do. The Lord often keeps his servants waiting, sometimes for a considerable time, before they are sure of his leading, and this waiting time can be difficult. It is not uncommon, in fact, for pastors to find themselves painfully perplexed. In the end, however, the prayed-for light is always given. God does not withhold it indefinitely and therefore we may wait for it patiently and expectantly.

This chapter is largely illustrative. The uncertainty that ministers have felt, the reasons for it, the pain that it has often given them, their confidence that the Lord would eventually make the path plain, the Scriptures that have comforted them; there is frequent reference to these things in ministers' biographies. The minister who is experiencing uncertainty himself is on a well-trodden path and will hopefully find help and comfort in the recorded experiences of some of his fellow travellers.

Reasons

Why the uncertainty? The answers to that are too numerous to list exhaustively. In one case there may be a single reason that looms very large in the pastor's thinking; in another case there may be a whole range of reasons. Only a few examples can be given.

One factor may be the *family*. In a helpful address entitled *When Should a Minister Leave a Church?* Derek Prime reminds us that one of the things that make the question of leaving so serious is the impact that the move will inevitably have on others. His first example is the family:

> If we are married, the decision plainly affects our wife. As our partner, where we go, she goes. Her happiness is bound up with ours; and vice versa. Being uprooted from friends may be more costly for our wife than for ourselves since we will find such considerations dwarfed by the challenge of a new sphere of service. If we have a young family, a change will affect our children, whether in terms of schooling, or, more important sometimes, their established friendships. The spiritual well-being of our children is an important consideration. Some church situations provide better opportunities than others for our children to make good friends with others of their own age.[1]

Is it at all surprising that, as a minister weighs such matters seriously, he should find himself uncertain as to whether a move would really be in the family's best interests?

Then there is the *church that the minister is being called to leave*. Who, for example, will take his place? When the Baptist pastor Spencer Cone was called in 1823 from Alexandria, Virginia, to a congregation in New York City this question of a successor greatly troubled him. 'The problem of a suitable replacement for him', writes his biographer, 'was a profound consideration.'[2] Properly so. A pastor who has his people on his heart and is all alive to their spiritual needs will inevitably be concerned that they should be well cared for in his absence. If, therefore, he has no colleague to step into his shoes and there is no immediate prospect of a replacement, he may well be uncertain as to whether it is right for him to leave.

His attachment to the congregation and its attachment to him can also generate uncertainty. He wrestles with whether it is really his duty to sever a bond so precious and strong. When Thomas Main of Kilmarnock was under call to Free St Mary's, Edinburgh, his elders and deacons wrote to him, urging him not to go and assuring him of their continued regard both for him and for his ministry. They looked upon him, they said, as their 'spiritual guide and instructor, a faithful watcher for souls, whose whole life and deportment' were consistent with his profession. 'Parents amongst us rejoice that you take so much interest in the young. The young look up to you with reverence, and yet with confidence and delight. The aged and infirm weary for your visits, and all the societies connected with the congregation cling to you as their centre.' His wife, who authored his memoir, adds that 'These and many other expressions of confidence rendered it extremely difficult for Mr. Main to break the tie.'[3]

The above reasons for uncertainty are weighty. But a consideration of much less intrinsic importance may create just as much uncertainty. When, after twelve years as pastor of a church in Mosgiel, New Zealand, the Revd F. W. Boreham was invited to Hobart in Tasmania, one serious difficulty for him was an act of kindness to him and his family by the Mosgiel congregation. In his delightful autobiography, *My Pilgrimage*, he writes that,

> three years earlier, in 1903, the church had made it possible for us, with our two little girls, to visit the Homeland [England]. In the goodness of their hearts they had granted us leave of absence for six months and had presented us with a substantial cheque towards the expenses of the tour. Would it be fair, after accepting so princely a gift at their hands, to lay down my charge?[4]

One further source of uncertainty may be *the church that has issued the call*. Spencer Cone, for example, when called to New York City, was not only troubled by the question of a successor to himself in Alexandria, but also by the fact that a significant minority in the calling church had opposed the call.

> Were they known? Were they resolutely against him or were they amenable to change? Would they stubbornly oppose his ministry among them or were they the type of people who could be won over by 'kindness and affection'? He was willing to come. The door seemed open. But he strongly desired to know the character and spirit of the opposers.[5]

The Revd William Arnot had a similar struggle. A call in 1862 to the Free High Church in Edinburgh had fallen through on account of the strong opposition of a portion of the congregation. When the call was being prosecuted anew the following year the opposition started up again. It 'caused him much anxiety and vexation', writes his daughter. Indeed, it was 'renewed and persisted in to such an extent that he felt inclined over and over again to interpose and authoritatively withdraw his name'.[6]

Pain

The resolution of the kind of uncertainties cited above can often be extremely difficult and at times can occasion no small amount of pain and perplexity. Many a moving testimony can be borne to this.

Writing to his friend Charles Brown, William Arnot confessed that, even after coming to the decision that it was right for him to accept the call to the Free High Church in Edinburgh, he found himself 'in almost complete darkness and desolation regarding it', and expressed the hope that 'God our Father will either open the path and shed light and hope on it, or alternatively make my stumbles the instruments of chastening me into conformity with the mind of Christ'. Later he added, 'We must work our way to the knowledge of the Lord's will through fire and water. He does not give it by large letters on the sky which the indolent might read.'[7]

It is very natural, however, to wish that in some such way the Lord *would* make his will clear. Speaking of his friend and colleague the Revd Matthew Dickie of Cumnock, Scotland, W. M. Taylor says,

> The good people of Cumnock were not long permitted to enjoy the services of their minister in peace. Other congregations heard of his fame as a preacher and his public spirit as a citizen, and coveted his gifts. Among these was the United Presbyterian Church, Canal Street, Paisley, which brought out a call in his favour, offering him a larger salary, and, what its members believed to be, a wider sphere of usefulness.

It occasioned him intense anxiety, in the midst of which he said to Taylor, 'What would I not give for a voice from heaven, to tell me what to do?'[8]

Other ministers have given us a similar insight into their perplexities—and the pain that can accompany it. On 3 August 1857, Thomas Main addressed the Presbytery of Irvine and indicated his willingness to accept the call to Free St Mary's, Edinburgh. Referring to the commissioners from his own congregation who had been arguing the case for retaining him in Kilmarnock, he said, 'I know that they will give me credit for sincerity; the struggle through which I have passed has well-nigh crushed and overwhelmed me.'[9] Hugh Heugh of Stirling, wrestling in 1821 with a call to Glasgow, wrote to his friend Dr Stark, 'It is impossible to express to you the anxiety that I feel. I am really at my wits' end. I never felt less composure.'[10] F. W. Boreham, after ten years' ministry in Hobart, Tasmania, accepted a call to Armadale in Australia. But it was 'after a month spent in a torture of indecision'.[11]

Confidence

Alongside the admissions of perplexity and pain, however, we find confidence being frequently expressed that the Lord, in his time and in his way, would make the path plain. After indicating his reasons for accepting the church in Armadale, for example, Boreham writes as follows:

> It is in my heart to offer one modest word of
> personal testimony. My pilgrimage has taught
> me many things; but it has made nothing more
> clear than the fact that, from those who humbly
> seek the leadership of the Kindly Light, the divine
> guidance is never withheld. In the course of my life
> I have had to make some momentous decisions—
> momentous to me—but, looking back along the
> road, I can now see clearly that, at every crisis, I
> was rightly led. Whenever the road forked, I heard
> a voice saying: '*This is the way, walk ye in it!*'[12]

Boreham himself had been deeply influenced as a young minister by an older friend and colleague in New Zealand, the Revd J. J. Doke. At the time when Boreham was in Mosgiel, under call to Hobart and unsure of what to do, he remembered for his comfort a conversation he had had with Doke during one of his visits to the Mosgiel manse:

> One lovely morning we were sitting together on the
> veranda, looking away across the golden plains to the
> purple and sunlit mountains, when I broached this
> very question: 'Can a man be quite sure,' I asked, 'that
> in the hour of perplexity, he will be rightly led? Can
> he feel secure against a false step?' I shall never forget
> his reply. He sprang from his deck-chair and came
> earnestly toward me. 'I am certain of it,' he exclaimed,
> 'if he will but *give God time*! Remember *that* as long as
> you live,' he added entreatingly. '*Give God time!*'[13]

J. H. Thornwell expresses a similar confidence that the Lord will guide. He is writing to his friend Dr Breckinridge and sympathizing with him in his difficulties: 'The circumstances in which you are placed must be full of embarrassment and perplexity. Broken in health, wounded in spirit, with two calls before you to different and responsible stations, you must feel very sensibly your need of Divine guidance and direction in guiding your steps.' After giving him some counsel, he proceeds to his own convictions on the matter: 'If we really desire, with an honest heart, to know our duty, and apply to God to be instructed by Him, He will impress upon the conscience a sense of duty, just in the direction in which He would have us to move, and which we shall feel it perilous to resist.' He continues, 'This sense of duty may be produced by some principle of the word which we perceive to be applicable to the exigency, or by an immediate operation upon the mind, which we are unable to explain.' He acknowledges that his friends sometimes charge him with 'a spice of fanaticism' for holding such views, but he is unmoved! 'This is my test,' he says, 'and I confess that, until after having sought from God, with simplicity and honesty, His divine direction, I feel such a sense of duty upon my conscience, such a "woe is me" upon the heart, I should feel it unsafe to move.' He concludes by saying, 'I am sure it is your purpose to glorify God, and I am equally sure that "the meek He will guide in His way."'[14]

We hear next from Thomas Boston. Writing of the time when he was called from Simprin to Ettrick, his biographer, Andrew Thomson, says, 'Like Moses in the wilderness, who would not move with his myriad host until the pillar of fire and cloud moved, he would take no step until Providence gave its sign.' Then he adds this personal testimony from Boston himself: 'The Lord helped me to believe that he would clear me in the matter in due time, and to depend on him for the same; while the word, "He that believeth shall not make haste", was helpful to me.'[15]

Finally, Hugh Heugh again. The call that he received to

Glasgow in 1821 was not the first one to that congregation. There had been one the previous year, and in the midst of his wrestlings with it he wrote thus to his friend Dr Mitchell:

> If I know myself, I have no other wish than this—to know the will of Him whom I desire to serve, and to whom, ere long, I must give an account. Could I only hear distinctly his voice, I think no tumult of feeling, no array of circumstances, would hinder me, in his strength, from obeying it. And I will not let go the confidence, which so many precious promises warrant me to encourage, and particularly this one which has been so dear to me—'I will lead the blind in a way that they know not.' I will not let go the confidence which such promises warrant, that amidst all my doubts and anxieties, God will guide me by his counsel.[16]

Preaching at a convocation of ministers of the Church of Scotland in November 1842, Dr Thomas Chalmers struck an identical note. His text was Psalm 112:4, 'Unto the upright there ariseth light in the darkness' (KJV). 'The great lesson of our text is,' he said, 'that if we purpose aright we shall be made to see aright, and that the integrity of our will shall be followed up by light in the understanding. God will not abandon to darkness those who cast their care and confidence upon Himself.' He concluded by saying, 'Ye men of God, who make the Bible the directory of your hearts and consciences, you will not long be left in uncertainty. He will make your way clear and open before you.'[17] Admittedly, Dr Chalmers was not addressing ministers who were unsure about what to do with a call to another congregation. But not only had these men come together at a time of great crisis in the Church, with the solemn possibility of the Church's connection with the state being broken up and with all the momentous consequences of a such a disruption looming large in their thinking; in many cases they were uncertain as to what to do. To men in such a position it is difficult to imagine a text and sermon more relevant. The application of them to the uncertainty of *this* chapter is just as apparent.

We end, however, with an example from Scripture itself. There came a point when the apostle Paul was sure that God had called him and his companions to cross from Troas to Macedonia and to preach the gospel there. It was an assurance, however, that had been long in coming. Between three and four hundred miles had been travelled—and not by car or plane!—and several other alternatives had been seriously considered before the uncertainty was over and the apostle was sure of the direction in which he and his companions were to go. They had first of all 'travelled throughout the region of Phrygia and Galatia, having been kept by the Holy Spirit from preaching the word in the province of Asia'. Then, 'When they came to the border of Mysia', they had tried to enter Bithynia, 'but the Spirit of Jesus would not allow them to'. Finally, they had come down to Troas, on the coast, and it was there, during the night, that Paul had his famous vision of the man of Macedonia standing and begging him to come over and help. It was the Lord's leading at last. 'After Paul had seen the vision,' writes Luke, 'we got ready at once to leave for Macedonia, concluding that God had called us to preach the gospel to them' (Acts 16:6–10).

They had taken a very long journey indeed, with several alternatives being considered on the way, with doors being closed in their faces, and doubtless much discussion among themselves and prayer to God for guidance, and still the uncertainty continued! But light was given eventually, and they were able to cross into Macedonia, confident that *this* was where God would have them go to preach his Word. And ministers today, facing similar uncertainty, may rest assured that to them too, if they will only wait and continue to seek the Lord, light will arise in their darkness and the direction in which they are to go will likewise become plain.

Some good reasons for staying

The evils of a change of field are many and serious, and only the most imperative reasons will justify a pastor in making it.

–Hezekiah Harvey

A minister who has received a call to another congregation needs carefully to consider the good reasons there may be for staying where he is and only take the decision to leave when he has done so. It is a point that scarcely needs to be argued. The sacredness of the bond between a pastor and his flock, the fact that he was originally placed over that flock by the Lord himself, the account that he must one day give to him for how he has cared for it, the possibilities for good or ill that a severance of the bond may have; all these and more make the decision regarding a call so serious that it ought only to be accepted when good reasons for *not* accepting it have been given the deepest consideration.

The family

We noted in the previous chapter that a pastor's uncertainty as to whether he should stay or leave may be rooted, at least in part, in *family considerations*. He asks himself, 'Would this move really be in my family's best interests?' and as he ponders that question he sees that there are excellent reasons for keeping his family where it is. His children are in good schools, they have a nice circle of friends, his wife enjoys her opportunities for service in the church, the family home is in a pleasant neighbourhood, they have put down roots and settled, etc; there is much to keep them where they are. It may still, of course, be the will of God that they leave. But as someone who is a husband and father *first*, a pastor cannot ignore these good reasons for staying—especially if he has reason to fear that in the new situation the losses will not be made up.

The congregation

In John 10 the Lord Jesus speaks about the hired hand who at a time of danger abandons the flock entrusted to his care: 'The hired hand is not the shepherd who owns the sheep. So when he sees the wolf coming, he abandons the sheep and runs away. Then the wolf attacks the flock and scatters it. The man runs away because he is a hired hand and cares nothing for the sheep' (vv. 12–13). Pastors, of course, do not *own* their flocks. But we have a solemn responsibility in our pastoral care to imitate the Shepherd who does. He loved the church enough to lay down his life for it, and we are bound in all our decisions to consult our congregations' highest interests, and especially to protect them against harm.

This has its obvious application to the issue of *a replacement for the pastor* should he leave. We saw in the previous chapter how Spencer Cone wrestled with this when under call to a church in New York City, and there is many a pastor who can identify with his concern. Consequently, one of the weightiest reasons for staying will always be the fact that it makes the question of a replacement disappear. The people can continue to enjoy the regular exposition of the Word, leadership and pastoral care to which they have been accustomed, and the pastor himself is relieved of all anxiety over his flock suffering by his departure. The likelihood of a long vacancy because of the scarcity of available men no longer needs to be considered. If the pastor has only one or two fellow elders, his staying will mean they will not have to bear the greatly increased burden that his departure would have imposed on them until another man was called to replace him.

Staying put will also mean that a pastor will retain what Hezekiah Harvey has termed 'the pastor's working capital',[1] namely, *his congregation's confidence and love*. These, says Harvey, 'constitute a chief element in his power'. Unlike 'mere popularity', they 'are only slowly acquired; but, once secured, they add immensely to the value of his public and private work'.

What an influence for good a pastor can have when his people love and trust him! But 'this advantage is all relinquished on leaving the field and must be again slowly acquired at another post'.[2] A pastor who considers just how much 'working capital' he has, and how long it has taken him to obtain it, and how much time and energy he will have to expend if he is to acquire it again in another situation, will want to be very sure that he has the Lord's call before moving on.

Then there is *the shortness of the time* that a man may have been with his church. A short ministry may, of course, be the Lord's will. And in the course of that short ministry a vast amount may have been accomplished. Paul's settled ministries, for instance, were short even at their longest—a year in Antioch, eighteen months in Corinth, three years in Ephesus. And yet how fruitful these ministries were! Nevertheless, the shortness of the time a man has been in a charge will often be a very good reason for staying where he is. After two or three years he may only be beginning to get to know his people well. New ministries that he has begun may still be in their infancy. The church may have been without a pastor for several years before he came and to be plunged so soon into the task of searching yet again may be very disheartening. If the pastor is a young man in his first church, the maturing of his gifts and the deepening and broadening of his ministerial experience may best be secured by a longer ministry. These and other considerations will often prevail upon a man to stay where he is and only seriously to consider leaving when he has been with his congregation for a more extended period.

Another reason a pastor may have for staying where he is is the awareness of *work that still remains to be done*. It is, of course, true that a Christian congregation is unendingly a work in progress (until the Lord returns!). There will always be things that remain to be done no matter how long a man is pastor and regardless of how hard he works and how much of the Lord's blessing is enjoyed. Problems to be resolved, the grieving to be comforted, backsliders to be restored, sins to be addressed, young Christians to be mentored, new leaders to be trained up, lost sinners to be reached, truths to be learned or re-learned; the list of things unfinished is always a long one!

Among them, however, may be some that the pastor feels it to be peculiarly important that he remain to address. It may, in fact, be a clear matter of duty that he remain. The prospect of leaving may be very attractive to him. There may be much in the calling church that appeals to him. He senses nevertheless that he must decline the invitation. There are things that seem imperatively to require his presence and he will not be like the hired hand of John 10 who runs out on the flock when the flock has a particular need of him. He will instead be like Titus (Titus 1:5), and remain where he is until these important matters are addressed.

Another factor pertaining to the congregation has to do with *the Lord's blessing*. When Paul was in Corinth, the Lord spoke to him in a vision one night: '"Do not be afraid: keep on speaking, do not be silent. For I am with you, and no one is going to attack and harm you, because I have many people in this city." So Paul stayed for a year and a half, teaching them the word of God' (Acts 18:9–11). The Lord had a particular reason for keeping the apostle in Corinth. There were many of his elect ones in the city and Paul's gospel ministry was to be the means by which he called them to himself. And so, with the prospect of future blessing (and the assurance of the Lord's protection as that prospect was realized), Paul remained in Corinth for a further eighteen months.

A pastor today may have no such explicit promise. But it may be that the call to another congregation comes to him at a time of special blessing in his own congregation; blessing that he may justifiably anticipate will continue. People in the community are being reached with the gospel in unusual numbers. There is a steady stream of conversions, a discernible movement of the Spirit among the young people, much of the presence of God in the worship services, the resolution of some long-standing difficulties among the members; it is an exciting time! How natural that a pastor should wish to remain where he is in such circumstances! And how necessary, perhaps, that he *should* remain so that he can give the church the wise guidance, the pastoral protection, the stable leadership and the discerning pulpit ministry that it needs if the Lord's blessing is to continue.

One further good reason for staying is *to spare the congregation sorrow*. In the mid-1550s the Scottish Reformer John Knox was in Geneva, ministering to a congregation of English refugees. He had the deepest affection for these men and women and could say that he would be content to end his days with them. Nevertheless, in the autumn of 1557, with the support of Calvin and his other colleagues, he said goodbye to them in order to return to Scotland. When he arrived in the French port of Dieppe, however, he found letters indicating that those who had extended the invitation in the first place had undergone a change of heart. Three days later a reply was on its way. It sheds a beautiful light on the affection in which he was held by his Geneva congregation.

> To some it may appear a small and light matter, that I have cast off, and as it were abandoned … my public office and charge [at Geneva] … committing that small, but to Christ dearly beloved, flock, over which I was appointed one of the ministers, to the charge of another. This to worldly men may appear a small matter, but to me it is such, that more worldly substance than I will express, could not have caused me willingly to behold the eyes of so many grave men weep at once for my cause, as I did in taking my last goodnight of them.[3]

The knowledge that a similar sorrow will attend his own departure is for many a pastor an excellent reason for staying where he is. He would spare his people that sorrow if he could.

It was for this very reason that the Revd John Fawcett, 18th-century pastor of a small and impoverished Baptist church in the northern England village of Wainsgate, changed his mind about leaving. He had accepted a call to Carter's Lane Baptist Church in London, but on the day of his departure the weeping of his people so moved both him and his wife that they could not bear to leave. It was out of this experience that Fawcett went on to write his lovely hymn 'Blest Be the Tie that Binds'.

The minister himself

Turning now to the minister himself, one factor inclining him to stay where he is may be *the breadth of the ministry that in God's providence he is exercising*. When Thomas Main was first approached about leaving Kilmarnock for Edinburgh, he wrote for advice to his friend Dr James Hamilton in London. In his reply Dr Hamilton 'said he felt great difficulty in giving an opinion. One circumstance which he seemed to think weighed against his leaving was, that evidently he was looked up to for advice by the younger ministers of the district.'[4] More than just the members of his congregation would be the losers if he left. A similar concern may rightly be felt (and expressed) when a minister is under call to a church in another country. If God has given him a preaching ministry considerably wider than that of his own church, the loss if he leaves will not merely be congregational but possibly national. And sensing that, a minister may conclude that, in the interests of this wider ministry (as well as in the interests of his particular flock), he ought to decline the call.

Then there is *the healthy pressure* of a continuing ministry on a man's choice of topics for preaching and study. Under the heading 'Evils of Change', Harvey writes,

> Few ministers widen their range of original
> investigation after their first pastorate. At the first
> post they are compelled to push out into new lines of

thought, but in a new field the temptation to use old subjects, if not old sermons, often proves irresistible, and their life-thinking is likely to move round in the same narrow range. Pastoral change often thus checks intellectual and theological growth.[5]

By remaining where he is, however, a minister is under the necessity of taking up books of Scripture or exploring Scripture themes that he has not tackled before, with all the fresh study that that requires. Or if he does go back over old ground he will need to endeavour to adopt a fresh approach.

A further reason for staying is *the discipline and growth that come by working through difficulties.* There are few things that make the prospect of a change more attractive than the existence of difficulties in a congregation. Division within the eldership, tensions between the minister and one of the deacons, unfair criticism, office-bearers or members who are downright hostile, disappointment over individuals who are resistant to admonition, deep-seated relational problems that defy resolution, poor attendance at prayer meetings, lack of conversions, people leaving the church; the list can go on and on. How heavily they can weigh on a man! What pain they can give him! How easy to want to be pastoring elsewhere—or even to be out of the ministry altogether!

Commenting on these difficulties, Harvey acknowledges that they 'enter more or less into every minister's lot', but advises that

> they may be no indication of duty to change. The trial may be sent as a discipline, designed to develop, through faith and patience, a nobler character and higher power in the pastor. Change in this case is only a cowardly running away from duty, and consequent failure to gain an intended blessing. Many a disruption of the pastoral tie, it may be feared, is thus only

> a shrinking from trial and its intended discipline,
> and results only in loss to pastor and people.[6]

Recognizing this, a pastor may come to the conclusion that the Lord's will for him is to stay where he is—hard as that may be. He needs to go on addressing the difficulties, looking to the Lord to strengthen him for the task and to bless his endeavours both to the congregation and to himself.

The same response may be called for when the difficulties *lie more with the minister himself.* His congregation may be in good heart and health but he himself is feeling tired, stale, even depressed, and for these reasons is ready to welcome the opportunity of making a fresh start somewhere else. It will often be the case, however, that these problems can be successfully addressed without the necessity of leaving his congregation. Perhaps he needs to work on his own relationship with the Lord because, in his zeal for the souls of others, he has been neglecting his own. Or perhaps he needs to be more disciplined about taking time off because, in defiance of the creation order, he has been working seven days a week and is physically and mentally run down. Maybe he just needs a good holiday or would benefit enormously from the refreshment and stimulation of a sabbatical.

A similar course of action may be called for when despondency results from *disappointment with the fruits of one's ministry.* Walter Chantry cites the case of Elijah:

> Elijah, at his crisis when fleeing in fear of Jezebel,
> definitely wanted to quit—even to die. However, after
> the Lord dealt with him *very* practically to strengthen
> his physical and emotional weakness with food and
> sleep he gave Elijah tasks which must be done before
> he would dismiss the prophet from office. Surely
> Elijah aimed too high in his expectations of success,

failed to see what God had done through him, and felt useless if he could not reach the heights he desired.[7]

It is often so with ministers still and the best solution to it will often be the same: not to leave, but to have a time of much-needed rest in which a more biblical and balanced perspective can be gained on their ministry.

A further reason for staying may be *the greater scope for the use of his gifts* that a man may have in his present charge. In early 1863 there was evidently some discussion between James Hamilton and William Arnot about a possible joint pastorate of Dr Hamilton's congregation in London. Arnot realized, however, that 'as long as both are able to preach twice every Sabbath, it would to the church appear strange that we should be reduced to half work. This objection seems very serious.'[8] At a certain stage in a man's ministry the prospect of a lighter workload may be an excellent reason for accepting a call. At other times it may be a temptation to be resisted. A minister who is in good health and who has full scope for the exercise of his preaching and teaching gifts may well conclude that he should stay where he is rather than accept a call to a congregation where the scope for such ministry is considerably less.

It is equally the case, however, that a good reason for staying may be the anticipation of *greater responsibility and a heavier workload* in the new congregation. While a man's age and state of health may fit him for his present charge he may have good reason to question whether on either or both of these grounds he would be wise to accept a charge that is going to make considerably more demands upon him. Health was one of the issues that Thomas Boston had to wrestle with when under call to move from Simprin to the larger and more demanding work at Ettrick. 'When the call came first to our presbytery, my health was sore broken: I looked rather like a man to be transported to eternity, than to another parish.'[9] A few days later he writes, '… it would appear unfair towards that parish for me to yield to take the charge of them under such bodily indisposition.'[10] Over against that was his conviction (and we would acknowledge it to be a correct one) that he ought not 'to shift that which otherwise appears duty, upon the account of bodily weakness and indisposition, but to be at the Lord's disposal, and hold even on the way, trusting him for strength for his own service'.[11] Age and health, however, are factors to weigh carefully, and it may be specifically with reference to them that the Lord will point out to us that our duty is to remain where we are.

The community

As a final good reason for staying we consider *the community to which the church belongs*. In the early years of James Stalker's ministry in St Brycedale Free Church, Kirkcaldy, Scotland, he had as a friend and near neighbour the Revd James Black of the Free Church in Dunnikier. In his *The Preacher and His Models* he gives the following touching reminiscence:

> It was my happiness, when I was ordained [1874], to be settled next neighbour to an aged and saintly minister. He was a man of competent scholarship, and had the reputation of having been in early life a powerful and popular preacher. But it was not to these gifts that he owed his unique influence. He moved through the town, with his white hair and somewhat staid and dignified demeanour, as a hallowing presence. His very passing in the street was a kind of benediction, and the people, as they looked after him, spoke of him to each other with affectionate veneration. Children were proud when he laid his hands on their heads, and they treasured the kindly words which he spoke to them. At funerals and other seasons of domestic solemnity his presence was sought by people of all

denominations. We who laboured along with him in the ministry felt that his mere existence in the community was an irresistible demonstration of Christianity and a tower of strength to every good cause. Yet he had not gained this position of influence by brilliant talents or great achievements or the pushing of ambition; for he was singularly modest, and would have been the last to credit himself with half the good he did. The whole mystery lay in this, that he had lived in the town for forty years a blameless life, and was known by everybody to be a godly and prayerful man. He was good enough to honour me with his friendship; and his example wrote deeply upon my mind these two convictions—that it may be of immense advantage to spend a whole lifetime in a single pastorate, and that the prime qualification for the ministry is goodness.[12]

Much, of course, will depend on the size of the community and the extent to which Christianity is respected within it. A city minister, for example, whose congregants are scattered far and wide and who himself lives at a considerable distance from the church building will inevitably find it a vastly greater challenge to influence his community for good than a rural minister whose people are all around him. A man who is wise, godly, kind and upright, however, and who remains for many years in the one place, and who becomes well known and respected there, may still come to have an influence for good that extends far beyond the members of his own congregation. And that is unquestionably an excellent reason for staying where he is.

Some good reasons for leaving

Chapter 5

A change of field is doubtless sometimes the duty of
a pastor, and the providence and Spirit of God,
which guided him in forming the pastoral relation,
will equally make plain the obligation to dissolve it.

–Hezekiah Harvey

I n his autobiography, F. W. Boreham tells us that he once heard
Dr A. T. Pierson advise his students 'never to leave one church
for another unless they felt both a propelling and an attracting
force at work. "Do not go," he said, "unless you distinctly feel
a hand pushing you out of your old sphere and distinctly see a
finger beckoning you to the new one!"' [1]

Without committing ourselves to the position that there are
always propelling *and* attracting forces at work when God is
calling a man to another church, experience would suggest
that that is *normally* the case. As he considers the matter
thoughtfully and prayerfully the minister sees good reasons
for moving on, both in the congregation he is being invited to
leave and in the congregation to which he is being called. The
object of this chapter is to examine what some of these good
reasons might be.

His present congregation

We begin with some factors pertaining to the congregation a
man is presently serving.

One of these may be *the difficulties that he is having to face*. We
noted in the last chapter that when difficulties arise in a church
it is frequently in both the pastor's and his congregation's best
interests for him to stay where he is and in the Lord's strength
to continue working away at them. It would be wrong to insist,
however, that difficulties must never be a reason for leaving.
The failure of even the most valiant efforts to put things right,
the worsening of the difficulties rather than their improvement,

the severity of the pain such situations bring to a pastor, the weariness they induce, their negative impact on his health or on his family; these may sadly become all-too-solid reasons for moving somewhere else.

In a section entitled 'Valid Reasons for Change', Harvey concedes, for example, that 'a minister, even after the most conscientious discharge of his duties, will sometimes find controlling influences in the church arrayed against him, or his cherished plans of church work defeated by counter-counsels; so that the pastor and permanent and influential members of the church are in relations wholly incompatible with comfort or efficiency'. The solution? 'If the relations cannot be altered, it would seem clearly his duty to leave, and to enter a field where his relations will be congenial and his labours unobstructed.'²

The difficulties become particularly acute when members or leaders move beyond obstructing a pastor to requiring things of him to which he cannot in good conscience agree. Is it insisted, for example, that he allow prophecy and tongues in public worship when he believes (rightly) that the tongues and prophecy of the New Testament are no longer conferred on the church? Or that he no longer preach on the sovereignty of God in election? Or that he must not freely offer Christ to everyone? When a pastor is deprived in this way of the liberty to lead his congregation biblically, he certainly has the soundest of reasons for accepting a charge in which this liberty will be enjoyed.

What about *the fewness of conversions*? It will often be the Lord's will that a minister who is seeing few, if any, conversions nevertheless presses on. He needs to remember that salvation is not a point but a line. It is an ongoing thing. God may not be greatly using him in the initiating of salvation, and yet, when it comes to the furtherance of that salvation in the lives of his people, he may be using him extensively. God is granting him a saving ministry!

However, in the light of our Saviour's statement in John 4 that the saying 'One sows and another reaps' (v. 37) is true, there may well come a point when the unfruitfulness of a ministry in terms of conversions makes it proper for a man seriously to consider a change. It has often happened that under a new ministry more conversions have taken place in a few months than in all the years of the previous pastor's ministry. The new pastor has reaped the benefits of his predecessor's labours (John 4:38). Who can deny that this is the doing of the Lord of the harvest and that he has moved one servant on and put another in his place for this very purpose?

Then there is the matter of *the pastor's health.* We noted in the previous chapter that the age and health of a pastor may be factors in determining him to stay where he is. He realizes that he may not be physically equal to the greater demands that the new work will make on him. It is also the case, however, that age and health may be the very things that render a change desirable or even necessary. The strain of ministerial work, continuing perhaps over many years, has taken its toll, physically, mentally, emotionally and even spiritually, and the pastor is drawn to a new charge because of the opportunity it affords of preserving (or restoring) his health and thereby lengthening his ministry.

In the memorial sketch of Thomas Main there is an interesting letter from Dr Alexander Duff, the well-known missionary to India. He is anxious to secure Main's services for India and argues this very point of health:

> Now, my dear friend, it has occurred to me
> forcibly that the very largeness of your Kilmarnock
> congregation must have tended to wear you out,
> and to render a change, in your case, desirable ...
> What then would you say to a call to Calcutta? ...
> You must have a huge stock of well-digested, as I
> know they are admirable, first-rate (pray excuse me)

sermons. They would all be new here, so that mental toil in your position here would be saved …[3]

There is always the danger, of course (and we were alerted to it by Hezekiah Harvey in Chapter 4), that recourse in a new pastorate to old sermon materials may be intellectually stultifying. Harvey acknowledges, however, that 'the severity of the draft made in this age on the intellect and nerves of a minister may sometimes compel change so as to obtain relief by the more free use of previous pulpit preparations. This, though unfortunate for the intellectual growth of the minister, is still to be chosen rather than broken health.'[4] Better to be preaching old sermons (though hopefully well revised) than to be disabled from preaching at all!

In the autumn of 1918 the threat of broken health was a key factor in inclining Kenneth MacRae to believe that his work as a Free Church of Scotland minister in the Argyllshire town of Lochgilphead was coming to a close and that he ought to accept a call to Kilmuir on the Isle of Skye.

> With three Sunday services in Lochgilphead, besides other congregations for which he was also responsible and to which he had to cycle long distances in all weathers, he felt that the labours required of him were verging on the superhuman. Physical ailments with which he had not previously been familiar began to worry him. [His] diary complains of 'tiredness' and 'exhaustion' … Occasionally when his physical condition was low he even wondered if his usefulness was near its end.[5]

The editor of MacRae's *Diary* tells us that later on, in his second pastorate in Kilmuir, health became a factor in leading him to consider a yet further move.[6]

What about the matter of *salary*? This is a delicate area in which a jealous watch over one's motives must be maintained.

The calling church may be offering a much larger salary than the one being presently received. Unquestionably, that can make a move attractive—especially if a man is struggling to make ends meet and provide adequately for his family. But is a larger salary a valid reason for moving? It cannot be ruled out. A minister ought to be candid with his fellow office-bearers or congregation and explain his difficulties. It may be that the church, because of its financially straitened circumstances, simply cannot pay him more—much as it would wish to. Alternatively, it may be just plain unwilling. In either case, if a minister on his present salary is facing genuine financial hardship and has no prospect of his situation improving, it is no dishonour to him to make salary a factor in his decision to leave. It is difficult, however, to disagree with Derek Prime's observation that 'such a consideration should never be the crucial factor in any move'.[7] We serve a God who is well able to provide for his servants.

A final consideration is *the benefit that the congregation itself may receive* through a change of ministry. Thomas Main, for example, in his address to the Free Presbytery of Irvine regarding his decision to leave Kilmarnock, said,

> … if I could have felt persuaded that it would have been, all things considered, for the lasting spiritual benefit of my people, that I should have spent the rest of my days among them, most gladly would I have done so. It is because I am convinced that a new ministry would be a benefit to them, that I am reconciled to the change. My heart tells me that on no inferior consideration could I ever have consented to it.[8]

In a later statement he returned to the theme: '… if I have not complied with your request to remain in my present sphere, it is because I felt persuaded, after the most anxious and prayerful consideration of the subject, that a new ministry would be a blessing to the people'.[9]

A man may feel, for instance, that if his people are to reach significantly deeper levels of maturity and Christian usefulness they need the freshness of a new ministry with its different emphases, gifts, graces and vision. This will often be the case with a man who has been in a congregation for a very long time. Again, he may perceive that his people have become too dependent on him and that they need to learn to depend more on the Lord. It will be good, therefore, for their faith to be tested as they wait upon the Lord for his provision. His leaving, too, will give opportunity for the development of preaching and leadership gifts in the congregation. It may also teach some who have undervalued the blessing of a regular expository ministry to prize it more when in God's kindness a new ministry begins. If a significant portion of the congregation has been unhappy with his ministry, his leaving will open the way for a new pastor to be called around whom the congregation will hopefully be able to unite.

His (potentially) future congregation

We turn now to consider some factors pertaining to the congregation to which a pastor is being called.

Sometimes it is *the attraction of its spiritual life*. In addition to his health struggles, one of the things which strongly inclined Kenneth MacRae to accept the call to Kilmuir was the much warmer spiritual atmosphere he sensed there than the one he was accustomed to in Argyllshire. He

> longed to be preaching in an area where there was
> a greater hunger for the Word of God and where
> there would be less occasion for the contentions
> which were necessary in Lochgilphead. In Kilmuir,
> in 1918, he felt that he was in a different atmosphere.
> There he visualized the possibilities of a spiritual
> quickening in a way which he could not do in the
> South. From that time on the 'pull' of the North

became irresistible—'I have desire, so great that to reject the call would be like cutting my hand off.'[10]

Of course, someone might ask: Is the attraction of warmer spiritual life really a valid reason for moving? Shouldn't a man just labour on where he is and continue to try to improve things in the congregation and community he is currently serving? Isn't that what Old Testament prophets like Jeremiah did? It *may* be his duty to stay. On the other hand the Lord, in his compassion for a minister who has laboured hard for his people and their community, and whose heart has been deeply affected by resistance to the truth (MacRae could write, for example, 'the worldliness, the materialism of Argyllshire is strangling me'[11]), may, for his servant's greater comfort and long-term usefulness, call him to a place where he will have a much more fruitful ministry and use the greater spiritual warmth of the place as the means by which he takes him there.

Sometimes, however, it is *the needs* of a place that constitute its attraction. The spiritual temperature is lower. There are far fewer who have true spiritual life. It is a very needy congregation and/or community. But that's the draw! Thomas Boston found it so when called from Simprin to Ettrick. In an endeavour to ascertain the divine will on the matter he visited Ettrick, preached there, and sought to make himself as thoroughly acquainted as he could with the moral and religious condition of the parish. 'Up to this time,' his biographer tells us,

> his heart's preference had been to remain in Simprin.
> But what he saw and heard during those days [in
> Ettrick] made him hesitate, and even incline to
> make it the object of his choice, not because his
> work would be easy, but because the crying wants
> of the people were so great. 'The desolation in that
> parish,' he says, 'ever since I saw it, hath great weight

on me, and I am convinced I should have more opportunity to do service for God there than here.'[12]

Then there is *the opportunity afforded for better use of a pastor's gifts*. For different reasons a pastor may find himself unable to exercise his gifts for ministry to anything like the extent that he would wish. The necessity of holding down another job, extra-congregational activities, numerous small (and sometimes not so small) tasks that in a larger church would fall to others; these can take up large quantities of time and energy he would rather devote to other and more important matters. A call to a congregation where he is going to have greater scope for the exercise of his gifts may be the very thing that he needs.

It was this situation that in 1916 made a move from Hobart in Tasmania to Armadale, a suburb of Melbourne, Australia, so attractive to F. W. Boreham. He says,

> Armadale exactly suited me. During my later years
> at Hobart, I often revolted against the necessity of
> attending such a multitude of meetings. I felt it my
> duty, as the representative of a central church, to
> take part in every helpful movement in the city. I was
> on every committee and was invited to speak at all
> kinds of public gatherings. This was all to the good;
> and, in a way, I revelled in it. But toward the end, I
> grudged the incessant drain upon my time and energy:
> I vowed that, if I ever left Hobart, it would be to
> assume a charge that would allow me to concentrate
> on preaching and writing. Armadale presented that
> coveted opportunity in a superlative degree.[13]

A fourth reason lies in *the wider scope for ministry and usefulness* that the new work offers. In 1913, commissioners from the Isle of Lewis argued this point in an effort to secure the translation of the Revd Kenneth Cameron from Skye to the Free Church of Scotland congregation in Stornoway:

It was the Church's 'plain duty to apportion their best men to the most populous and urgent parts'. 'Stornoway', they pleaded, 'was the commercial capital of the Western Isles, with a fluctuating population of 4000 to 7000 people; the finest school in the West, with about 800 pupils; and a secondary school with about 200 students, the majority of whom are Free Church. How were our Highland pulpits to be filled with ministers? Not from Canada or Ireland, but, as of old, from the homes of our Free Church people. In the interests of the Church as a whole, Stornoway offers a fine field for Mr. Cameron's talents and piety—a splendid nursery to prepare Free Church students.'[14]

In *St Brycedale Church, Kirkcaldy: The Origin and History of St Brycedale Church*, there is a fascinating letter addressed to his office-bearers by James Stalker, outlining his reasons for accepting a call in 1887 to Free St Matthew's, Glasgow, after a ministry of twelve years in Kirkcaldy. One paragraph touches on this very subject of a wider field of usefulness—this time from the perspective of the minister being called to it. He writes,

> I have seldom indeed received any invitation to go elsewhere which has been much of a temptation to me. Outsiders do not know the importance of St. Brycedale, but I have always had the highest idea of it. The size of our congregation, the composition of its membership, its place in the town and its influence in the county, all give it a unique character; and I would not think of going from it except to work still more important. There seems to me, however, to be even more important work to do in Glasgow. I have received a letter from our students there, urging me to consider the 100,000 young men in the city. I do not expect to have less work, or more comfort there; quite the opposite. Professor

> Drummond wrote me the other day, saying, 'Glasgow is the best place in the world for a man who wishes to do service to his Church and fellow men; this is its one attraction, it has no other.' It is with this before my eyes that I should like to go. St. Matthew's is at present in many respects inferior to St. Brycedale, but it is in the centre of the work, and this is its attraction for me.[15]

Harvey goes so far as to make removal to a wider field a matter of *duty* for some men. In the section 'Valid Reasons for Change' referred to above he gives as his first reason,

> Growth in pulpit and pastoral power beyond the scope of the field. A young man has settled, perhaps, in a circumscribed field. Fidelity in study and labour has developed him, so that his capacity plainly fits him for a wider sphere. If this is made evident by the judgement of his brethren and the providence of God, he is required by duty, alike to his own life-usefulness and to the cause of Christ, to enter the wider field opened before him.[16]

There is a great need, however, for caution here. It was precisely this kind of argumentation (applied, however, to an older man) that hastened the death in 1847 of one of the most remarkable ministers of the Scottish church—the Revd Alexander Stewart of Cromarty. There was intense pressure on him to move from his quiet village charge to the city of Edinburgh, and the conflict that it created was so tremendous as to fatally undermine his health. He was, as the moving inscription on his tombstone puts it, 'invincibly attached to the retirement and obscurity' of his situation.

> Cleaving also to his flock with an affection which time seemed to increase, his sensitive nature shrank from the honours and the responsibilities which the Church repeatedly sought to lay upon him; and

when at length chosen to be minister of Free St.
George's, Edinburgh, and about to be translated
to that important charge, the Lord, pitying the
perplexities of his spirit, put an end to them by
suddenly removing him to the upper sanctuary.[17]

What to us may seem clear duty may not be so in the eyes of the
Lord, and we must beware of putting undue pressure on men to
move to a larger work when in fact it may be best for them, for a
number of reasons, to stay where they are.

Nevertheless, it may well be for this wider sphere of ministry
and usefulness that the Lord has been preparing the man. The
experiences through which he has passed, the maturity and
knowledge that he has gained, the development of pulpit gift
and pastoral wisdom that there has been, may have all been
with a view, in the Lord's purpose, to equipping him for this
more responsible and influential charge. In prayer and through
consultation with others it needs to be ascertained if this is so.
And if it is, then it clearly *is* his duty to go.

Decision
time

I have looked at the subject from every side, and had the benefit of so much advice that I should think no consideration of any importance can have escaped me.

–James Stalker

Once a call has been issued an answer, of course, must eventually be given. The purpose of this chapter is to lay down some general principles in regard to making, implementing and reviewing this decision. How should the matter be approached? Our answer will take the form of seven exhortations.

Take your time!

F. W. Boreham's translation from Hobart to Armadale was, as we saw in the previous chapter, from a situation where he was overwhelmed with extra-congregational activities to one where he could focus his attention on preaching and writing. Interestingly, however, when the call came, his initial inclination was to turn it down. 'At first,' he writes,

> the project seemed unthinkable. How could I tear myself away from Hobart? How could I leave the people who were doing everything in their power to nurse me back to health? [He was recovering from a long illness at the time.] I was actually drafting a telegram declining the call when the Rev. Archibald G. Brown, formerly of the East London Tabernacle, intervened. Mr. Brown had been living for some months at Hobart and we had all become very fond of him. He strongly urged me to take my time.
>
> 'Do not reply in a hurry,' he pleaded. 'It is by no means clear that your health will permit you to resume the burden of your work here. A change

might work wonders. And if you are to have a change, what could be better than Armadale? It is one of the most beautiful churches in Australia; it is splendidly officered and highly organized; you would be relieved of all administrative details; you would have a magnificent preaching opportunity; ample scope would be given you for your literary work; make quite sure that you are acting in harmony with the will of God before you finally decline!'[1]

The same counsel ought surely to be followed when the inclination is to *accept*. Take your time!—even if to accept the call seems self-evidently the right thing to do. It is always the wisest course deliberately to pause, ponder and pray; to weigh everything up; to consult with others; to listen to others; to consider the reasons *against* as well as *for* leaving; and only to conclude that it really *is* the will of God for you to go when, after every test, that remains your conviction.

Reference was made in Chapter 1 to what Thomas Chalmers did when anticipating a call from Kilmany to Glasgow. He put down on a sheet of paper, in parallel columns, his arguments for leaving and for staying.[2] The details do not concern us, but rather the wisdom of the procedure. To do what we have been doing in the previous two chapters—to consider the alternatives carefully—is an excellent antidote to over-hastiness! Of especial interest is how Chalmers concluded. At the bottom of each column he responded to his observations with a separate written prayer: imploring the Lord to guide him; to help him if he should go to Glasgow; to bless the people among whom he had been labouring; etc. He was a man who was taking his time—and doing so *prayerfully*.

Chalmers' prayerfulness needs to be noted carefully. 'We rather assume', writes Iain D. Campbell, 'that ministers are in a spiritually healthy condition, and therefore open to knowing the will of God.'[3] A minister under call needs to ask himself if, in his own case, that assumption is warranted. Is he weighing everything up in an atmosphere of prayer? Is his careful examination of this new call being truly done before the Lord? In this connection it is instructive to note what was happening in Antioch in Acts 13, when the Lord made known his will regarding Saul and Barnabas. They and other church leaders were 'worshipping the Lord and fasting' (v. 2). 'Luke clearly wants us to see a connection between the worship, prayer, and fasting on the one hand, and the decisive guidance of the Holy Spirit on the other: "While they were fasting, the Holy Spirit said." This is a significant biblical precedent for engaging in worship-fasting-prayer in the earnest pursuit of God's will for our lives and the life of our church.'[4]

Find out all you can!

Depending on the search procedure adopted by the calling church there may be ample time for this before a call is issued. Certainly, it needs to happen before the call is accepted. The church is presumably finding out all that it can about the man whom it is considering. That should be met by an equal thoroughness in finding out everything about the church.

The church's Constitution, for example, should be studied with the utmost care. So too its doctrinal statement. If subscription is required to one of the historic Confessions of Faith, enquiry should be made as to the exact terms of subscription. There should be complete honesty about any areas of the Confession with which one is in disagreement, and a satisfactory answer obtained to the question whether such disagreement is acceptable. What about the church's *own* subscription to the Confession? Are there areas of disagreement that *it* has? Then there are the extra-Confessional issues. Is there liberty to hold and to preach one's convictions about matters not covered by the Confession? Or are there certain positions that the church has adopted—on women deacons, for example—which, though not covered by the Confession, it would expect its minister to hold to (or at least abide by)?

There may, of course, be no Confession of Faith but just a general statement covering basic evangelical beliefs. If so, the enquiry into what else the church believes, what it expects its pastor to teach, and what liberty he himself has in his preaching, is of massive importance. If he is a Calvinist, will he have freedom to preach on election and efficacious grace? Similarly, if he is a cessationist in regard to charismatic gifts. And what about the thorny issue of eschatology?

The list could go on and on. The church's recent history, its practice of discipline, its position on worship, its missionaries and how it oversees them, its current spiritual health, the extent of its unity, the relationships among its elders, the level of commitment both of its members and of its office-bearers, how it has treated its former pastor, why he himself has left (or is leaving); these are all areas into which it is wise to make enquiry. Our questioning, indeed, should be as exhaustive as we can make it. There ought to be nothing into which we are afraid to probe. Acceptance of a call should be made on the basis of as complete a knowledge of the calling congregation as it is possible to obtain. It goes without saying that this will not in itself guarantee a successful ministry. But it will help to avoid the pain of a pastoral relationship getting into difficulties, or the tragedy of that relationship falling apart, over things that could (and should) have been known beforehand.

Listen to others!

'In the multitude of counselors there is safety' (Prov. 11:14, NKJV). A pastor who is under call will do well, then, to listen carefully to what spiritually minded men (and women) have to say about the matter, to sift their counsel thoroughly and prayerfully, and to make his decision in the light of it.

The judgements of others will sometimes be presented to him formally. It is a time-honoured tradition in Presbyterianism, for example (at least in Scotland), for representatives both of the congregation issuing the call and of the congregation whose minister has received the call to appear before the bar of the minister's Presbytery. There, in the minister's presence, and in that order, they give their reasons, first, why he should be translated to the calling church and, second, why he should stay where he is.

With equal formality there may be letters from a minister's fellow elders, or from his deacons, giving their considered judgement on the matter. At an informal level, there will inevitably be letters and emails from individual members, colleagues, friends and family members that do the same thing. A wise minister will consider all this counsel carefully.

He himself will be well advised to *seek* counsel by approaching those whose judgement is worthy of respect and who may be expected to be honest with him, and by asking their opinion: his fellow elders, for example; other ministers; in certain circumstances, his doctor. He might consult someone who has no connection with the calling congregation but who is familiar with it, or someone who is independent of his own congregation but is well acquainted with *it*. What do *they* think?

In the light of all this counsel it may become (or remain) a man's conviction that he ought to *leave* his congregation. Writing to his office-bearers regarding his call in 1887 to Free St Matthew's in Glasgow, James Stalker, for example, said,

> I have looked at the subject from every side, and had the benefit of so much advice that I should think no consideration of any importance can have escaped me. The deputation from the Deacons' Court that waited on me last week set the case for St. Brycedale before me in a very cogent and affecting way; and I must have been made of stone if I had not been deeply moved by

> the demonstration which Mr. Nairn's remarks called
> forth at the meeting last night ... [Nevertheless,] It
> is with a heavy heart that I announce to you that the
> decision I have come to is that I should go to Glasgow.[5]

Alternatively, the representations made may persuade a minister that he ought to *stay*. William Arnot, minister of Free St Peter's, Glasgow, in the 1860s, had made no secret of his convictions about one day leaving his congregation: 'Publicly and privately, for many years, I have made known my judgement, that what remains of my ministry would probably be fresher and more effective for myself and the church, if it were exercised in a new sphere.' Accordingly, when an opportunity came to minister to another Glasgow congregation, he 'entertained and expressed an inclination to close with the invitation'. He tells us, however, that his 'people resisted and overcame that inclination, mainly on the ground that the place was too near (exactly two miles), and would shatter St. Peter's'.[6]

Whatever the outcome, it will be good to have had the involvement of others in the decision-making process. 'Corporate guidance', writes Derek Prime, 'is safer than personal conviction, and confirms the latter when it is right.'[7]

Let the decision be taken for you!

It was the practice in the General Associate Synod (one of the branches of the Secession Church in Scotland) for the Synod itself to make the decision in the case of a newly licensed minister receiving a call to more than one congregation. In May 1806, for example, judgement was given in the case of Hugh Heugh who was under call to three congregations. 'After long deliberation and special prayer, it was carried in the Synod that he should be ordained in Stirling [one of the three calling congregations]. This decision, formed on public grounds, was in accordance with his own desires.'[8]

It was also the Secession rule that when a call came to a

minister already in a charge the responsibility for making the decision lay, again, not with the one called but with the church courts. Thus, when over a two-year period, 1819–1821, Heugh was called three times from Stirling to the same congregation in Glasgow, it was the Synod on each occasion that took the decision—twice refusing translation, the third time granting it (and only then after a debate lasting eight hours and by a majority of two!).

Heugh's biographer tells us that the Secession's rule on this matter was one 'to the alteration of which, Mr. Heugh, and many others were decidedly opposed'.[9] In a letter written at the time of the first call, for example, he says,

> The trying question comes—What is to be done? I should be extremely sorry to think that its determination should rest with me; the responsibility connected with which, I should feel most dreadfully. And, indeed, it does not become me to take it, since with us, it formally belongs to the courts. My opinion has always been, that the preacher or minister, being a party, should be heard—that while he should not be compelled to speak his mind, he should have the opportunity—and that the judges should attach what weight they think proper to his language or to his silence. But I have never thought that the question should be settled betwixt the candidate and the people, nor even that his voice should decide the matter.[10]

His biographer adds, 'His main relief [given his feelings of uncertainty over whether it was his duty to stay or leave] had always been a conviction that the chief responsibility connected with the decision was not with him.'[11] It was a comfort, too, when in 1821 the Synod decided in favour of Glasgow, and he had a sorrowful farewell to take to his people in Stirling, to be able to trace the *divine* hand in it all: 'Over these arrangements ["which", he says, "were made without any agency of mine"] the Lord of the church has presided, and his grace is sufficient for me.'[12]

Secession practice eventually changed. The last case in which the Synod exercised what has been finely called 'its ancient constitutional power to direct the settlement of its ministers'[13] was in September 1833 when it was agreed without a vote to permit the Revd David King to leave his charge in Dalkeith, near Edinburgh, for a Secession congregation in Glasgow. The new arrangement undoubtedly had its advantages. But men in the agonies of perplexity missed the old arrangement. The Revd John Edmond of Glasgow, for example, writing in the early 1850s after an almost unbearably painful experience of decision-making, says,

> I cannot help thinking that it would be well if the church could relieve her ministers of the grievous burden of deciding on their own sole responsibility the question of duty in the case of translating calls. There are difficulties, it is acknowledged, connected with any other regulations than those now obtaining; but not to speak of various disadvantages of a different description connected with the present plan, its propriety would need to be very clear to warrant the imposing on individual consciences and hearts of so severe a task.[14]

Within the Free Church of Scotland a minister in perplexity over the right decision to take has the *option* of placing the matter in the hands of his fellow Presbyters. There was an instance of this in 2003 when the Revd Iver Martin was called from Bon Accord Free Church in Aberdeen to the Free Church congregation in Stornoway. Writing of the Presbytery meeting when the matter of the call was taken up, he says,

> The meeting was a very special one. The two men
> from Stornoway who had been selected to bring the
> call to the Presbytery spoke very powerfully and the

> two men who had been selected to try to keep me in
> Aberdeen responded as best they could. I was then
> asked for my response and I told the Presbytery that
> because I found it so impossible to come to a decision
> I was going to place the decision into their hands.[15]

He had wrestled with the matter for three months and still had no
clear sense of God's leading. The Presbytery, after earnest prayer
for God's guidance, voted in favour of him accepting the call.

Reflecting on the decision Martin says, 'the weight of uncertainty
was gone and for me there was no sense of "have I done the right
thing?" I felt a sense of definitiveness which I don't think there
might have been had I come to the conclusion by myself.' He
adds, 'I believe that after praying about a call where there is no
clear way ahead, there are two options. One is to stay where you
are, there being no clear guidance to move; *or* place the matter in
the hands of the wider church and submit to their consensus.'[16]

Many ministers, uncertain of what to do with a call, have,
of course, no Presbytery of godly men to whom to submit such
a question. But where they do, there is much to commend the
practice. It is clear, for example, from the instances of Titus
and Timothy moving on Paul's instructions that, in principle,
a minister's decision to move from one place to another may
properly be taken by those who have lawful authority over him.
Paul himself, in Acts 13, had the will of God that he leave Antioch
for missionary work made known to him through his fellow
church leaders. Presbyterian practice also gives expression to
the concept of a church unity that is broader than that of the
individual congregation, and it enables a man to enjoy the safety
that lies in a multitude of counsellors (Prov. 11:14). And where
there is *no* Presbytery? In his uncertainty it is lawful for a man
to take a similar course to that of his Presbyterian brother and
to place the matter either in the hands of his fellow elders (or
deacons) or in the hands of the congregation as a whole.

Avoid being insensitive!

We come now to the question of how and when the fact of a call (and especially the decision to accept it) should be communicated to a minister's fellow office-bearers and his congregation. We begin with the negative. James Taylor writes,

> Stories abound, some of them bordering on the horrific, which illustrate how it ought not to be done. Most of them involve a measure of dishonesty, lack of integrity and just plain deceit. One colleague informed his unsuspecting congregation that he had been invited to preach in a large overseas church. He assured them that it had a pastor. What he did not tell them was that it was a pastor emeritus. He then arranged for a supply preacher to read the bombshell of his resignation to his bewildered people ... Such behaviour does little to commend the dignity of the pastorate or honour the Lord who calls.[17]

How, then, *ought* it to be done? Opinions will inevitably differ on details. When F. W. Boreham, for example, was called in 1906 from Mosgiel to Hobart he told no one. 'If my call to Hobart had been public property,' he writes, 'I could have consulted my officers on the point [the reference is to a difficulty that he had in accepting the call]. But not a soul knew of it, and we thought it best to keep the secret to ourselves until the decision had been taken.'[18]

Other men will inevitably take a different approach and will want closely to involve at least their fellow officers in the decision-making process, perhaps at a fairly early point. Much will depend on the relationship that a minister has with these men, the degree to which the call is already public knowledge, and whether there are circumstances in the church that make a change particularly desirable. Regardless of the details, however, we should be at pains to avoid being insensitive. We are to be pastors after the pattern of the Good Shepherd himself and to love deeply the flock over which he has placed us. Such love dictates that we break the news of the call, and especially of our decision to leave, with the utmost sensitivity to the feelings of the people, with a desire to minimize pain, and in a way that is calculated to do good and not harm.

Have the courage to reverse the decision!

In December 1845, Dr J. H. Thornwell wrote a long letter to his friend Dr Breckinridge, carefully explaining the circumstances that now made it impossible for him (Thornwell) to become pastor of the church in Baltimore whose call he had accepted. In the course of the letter he gives a brief apology for a minister reversing his decision on a call when no longer convinced that he has the Lord's leading to go.

A pastor 'is bound', he says, 'to do what *seems* to be the will of God; and if, after the acceptance of a call, circumstances should arise to change his impressions of the leadings of Providence, he is bound to withdraw that acceptance. The whole matter is open for new light, until the pastoral relation has actually been established.'

Thornwell then brings the calling church into the equation as well:

> A church, in calling a pastor, endeavours to obey the will of God; a pastor, in accepting, aims at the same rule. They both follow the indications of Providence, and their mutual acts are formal expressions of the light in which they regard those indications. Now, should anything transpire which marks this conclusion as evidently *repugnant* to the Divine will, the matter is ended; no obligation exists on either side, except to follow the clearest light.[19]

It is unnecessary to go into the question of what those things are that could call for a reversal of the decision. It is the principle itself that is important. A pastor accepts a call because he believes that he has the Lord's leading to do so. If he should afterwards discover that he was mistaken, or should circumstances so alter as to make it clear that it would be wrong for him now to go, let him have the courage to reverse the decision! Better the pain, the embarrassment perhaps, the possible misunderstandings and recriminations, than to go ahead and consummate the call when one is sure that that is actually the wrong thing to do.

The same rule applies when the mistake lies not in the acceptance of the call but in its refusal. A pastor realizes, for whatever reason, that he ought not to have said 'no'. It may not be possible, of course, to remedy the situation. But if it is, let him have the courage to reverse the decision! Better to acknowledge that one has been in error and to indicate that there is now a willingness to accept the call than to remain silent and permit pride and feelings of shame to perpetuate the error.

Trust the Lord!

We end by again taking up the theme with which Chapter 3 concluded—the confidence we may have that the Lord will clear away our uncertainties and grant us the guidance we need. To illustrate, we return to F. W. Boreham and his difficulty in making the decision to leave Mosgiel for Hobart. It lay, as we saw in Chapter 3, in a matter of no great intrinsic importance. The church had generously made it possible for him and his family to visit England three years earlier. Would it be fair to leave them having received such a gift? The story of how that difficulty was resolved, setting him free, in good conscience, to accept the call, is a remarkable commentary on how completely we may trust the Lord for necessary light. It is told in his own words.

> For reasons of their own, the officials at Hobart
> had asked me to let them have my decision not
> later than Saturday, March 24, and I had promised
> to respect their wishes in that matter. As that day
> drew nearer, the issues narrowed themselves down

to one. Did the acceptance of the English trip commit me to a prolonged ministry at Mosgiel?

When that Saturday dawned, we were as far from finality as ever. The post office closed at five o'clock in the afternoon and I was determined, come what might, to hand in my reply by then … That Saturday afternoon, to add to our distress, a visitor arrived. She stayed until half-past four.

'Come on,' I said to my wife, 'put on your hat and we'll walk down to the post office. We must send the telegram by five o'clock, whatever happens.' At five minutes to five we were standing together in the porch of the post office, desperately endeavouring to make up our minds. We were giving God time: would the guidance come? At three minutes to five, Gavin, the church secretary, rode up on a bicycle. He was obviously agitated. 'What do you think I heard in the city this morning?' he asked eagerly. I assured him that I could form no idea. 'Well,' he replied, his news positively sizzling on his tongue, 'I heard that you have been called to Hobart!' 'It's true enough, Gavin,' I answered, 'but how can we consider such an invitation after your goodness in giving us a trip to England?' 'A trip to England!' he almost shouted. 'Man alive, didn't you earn your trip to England before you went? Why, you're very nearly ready for another!' I begged him to excuse me for a moment. The clerk at the counter was preparing to close the office. I handed in my telegram and rejoined Gavin …[20]

Later, at Gavin's house, Boreham wrote out his resignation.

Wasn't he taken right to the edge? But the guidance came at last! So it will for us, if we will only wait for it. In some way or other, the Lord will make the path plain. Trust him!

What will the change be like?

I do not pitch my expectations in the same high key as some of those who have called me; for I know how weak my powers are in comparison with the work needing to be done. But a step like this has to be taken in faith …

–James Stalker

The decision has been taken and, as the chapter title implies, it is to leave. The call has been accepted. The pastor and his family are now entering a period of major change. What is it going to be like? Our final chapter will reflect on some aspects of the answer to that question. It will hopefully serve both to caution us against unrealistic expectations and, at the same time, to encourage us with the certainty of the Lord's blessing in the new work.

The sorrow of parting

Before the new work begins, however, the old work must end and goodbyes be said. It can be an extraordinarily painful thing. We saw in a previous chapter that it was this that constrained John Fawcett to alter his decision for London and stay with his small flock in Wainsgate. The sorrow at the time of his leaving so affected him that he could not bring himself to go. Few pastors will do as Fawcett did—much as they admire and sympathize with his feelings. They will follow through with their decision to leave. But it will more often than not be with very sore hearts.

Sorrow at parting is, of course, a thing of degrees and reflects the closeness of the bond between pastor and people, something that in turn is determined by the length of time they have been together, how happy a pastorate it has been, and how difficult or otherwise have been the circumstances preceding and contributing to the move. At one extreme, the sorrow may be virtually non-existent because the relationship between pastor and people has so broken down. At the other extreme, it may be so acute as to be almost unbearable.

When Kenneth MacRae left his first pastorate in Lochgilphead it was with mixed feelings. On the one hand, in anticipation of the parting, he could write in his diary, 'I love my dear congregation, and to leave them tears at my heart-strings.' In a similar vein, he writes of his final service, 'Felt it a great ordeal.' And yet, as the editor of his diary notes, 'when the time of parting came on the Tuesday following, it was with a sense of the coldness of the place he was leaving behind and relief to be gone'.[1]

There were no such mixed feelings when Thomas Chalmers left Kilmany for Glasgow in 1815. His biographer, William Hanna, says that

> the two chief obstacles to Mr. Chalmers' removal from Kilmany were his fears as to the amount of extra and unprofessional labour which was laid upon the clergymen of Glasgow, and his regrets at leaving a people and neighbourhood to which he was very tenderly attached. An explanatory letter from Dr. Balfour helped to remove the one; it cost acute and long-continued suffering to remove the other ... Coming back to his parish, more than twenty years after he had left it, he exclaimed, 'Oh! there was more tearing of the heart-strings at leaving the valley of Kilmany than at leaving all my great parish at Glasgow.'[2]

His diary entries of the time bear that out. 'My tenderness', he writes in one entry, 'has risen to all the agony of a passion.' In another, 'I am in great heaviness.'[3]

The Revd Adam Forman, minister first at Innerwick in East Lothian, Scotland, and afterwards, from 1844, of the Free Church of Scotland congregation of Leven in Fife, went through similarly deep waters. His experience illustrates the long-continued hold that a much-loved congregation can have on a pastor's heart:

> It was only after a very severe struggle, and under the pressure of the strongest arguments, that he could make up his mind to leave a spot where for twenty years he had so faithfully laboured, and which had become inexpressibly dear to him by many sacred, and also by several sad associations. His people affectionately clung to him, and it was almost a mortal agony for him to tear himself away from them and remove to another part of the vineyard. The principle of local attachment seemed to operate on him with peculiar power. Often, after he was settled at Leven, and was deservedly endeared to his new flock, he would, in a fit of pensive meditation, walk up to the higher grounds whence he could look across the sea, and gaze with wistful eyes on the opposite coast, where in the extremity of East Lothian, rose the hills of Innerwick.[4]

The relish of a new beginning

Sorrow, however, is only one side of the experience of parting. Along with it (in most cases) there is also pleasure, even excitement, at the prospect of a new pastorate. One element of this is the opportunity now afforded for a fresh beginning. This was evidently a factor in James Stalker's decision to leave Kirkcaldy for Glasgow in 1887. To quote again from his letter to his fellow officers:

> … ours is too large a congregation for a man to begin in immediately after leaving College, as I did, and continue in for the rest of his life. I have felt the strain to be heavy all along; and, although as yet I may in some degree have been equal to it, I feel it would be an immense relief to make a new beginning elsewhere,

with all the accumulations of the last twelve years. I
do not mean merely that I might perhaps preach some
of my sermons over again; but my store of ideas and
experience would be all fresh to another congregation;
and a minister has quite a different feeling in giving
forth what is fresh to his hearers from that which he
has in repeating what his hearers already know.[5]

The anticipation of this new beginning will often serve to
mitigate the pain of parting. The actual experience of it may
do the same. This was certainly what F. W. Boreham found
when he moved from Mosgiel in New Zealand to Hobart in
Tasmania:

It was at Hobart that I found myself. From the
moment at which I entered the pulpit for the first time
I realized that I was preaching with a confidence and
enjoyment that made my ministry a perfect revelry.
It was a wonderful experience to be starting afresh
with no old ghosts to haunt me. In the course of a
long first pastorate, a man makes all sorts of mistakes,
the repercussions of which cramp his movements
at every turn. He changes his mind on a variety of
subjects and finds the expression of his earlier opinions
quoted to him to confound his enunciations of his
later and riper judgements. And there is infinite relish
in being able to say whatever is in your heart to say
without having to ask yourself how recently you
have said something of the same kind. When once
I had survived the wrench of tearing up my roots at
Mosgiel, and outlived the ordeal of seeing new faces
and hearing strange voices, I discovered that the
joys of making a new beginning were immeasurably
greater than I had for a moment suspected.[6]

Difficulties

It is important at this point, however, to strike a cautionary note. One of the purposes of this chapter is to try to guard pastors against unrealistic expectations and it is all too easy for passages such as the above by Stalker and Boreham to generate them. That is by no means to fault these men for what they wrote. It is proper to relish a new beginning and to revel in it when it is given. But our eager anticipations as we consider what a change will be like need to be tempered by the reality of future *difficulties*. Take the following three examples:

MATTHEW DICKIE

For the first two years after leaving Cumnock for a new pastorate in Bristol, England, things went well for Matthew Dickie. It was a new work and the growth of the congregation was most encouraging. A church building was erected and on 7 September 1859 it was formally opened for public worship. Dickie's biographer, his close friend W. M. Taylor, writes that 'within a fortnight … almost all the sittings were let, and everything seemed to be in the highest degree satisfactory'. It marked the beginnings, however, of a great trial:

> [T]he church, though exceedingly beautiful, was found to be acoustically bad, and in a short time a great number of the sittings were given up, because their occupants could not distinctly hear the preacher's voice. Many devices were tried to remedy this effect. The pulpit was brought forward, and a wooden pulpit with a canopy was erected, but with little effect. At length, by the alteration of the position of the pulpit, and the hanging of the walls with thick crimson cloth, the evil was in a great measure remedied; but this was only after a fearful expenditure of vital energy, and many protracted periods of deep depression on the part of the minister. One of his first elders, who

had by that time removed to London, told him that
the cause lay not in the building, but in his voice, and
this so greatly distressed him that his health was,
for the time, seriously impaired. Indeed, his medical
friends did not hesitate to affirm that by the efforts
which he made to surmount this difficulty, and the
mental anxiety which its existence caused, his last
illness was both precipitated and aggravated.[7]

THOMAS BOSTON

With Thomas Boston the problem lay not with the building
(though one of the trials he did have to face when he moved
from Simprin to Ettrick was the ruinous condition of the manse)
but with the people. In his first charge he had witnessed a
remarkable work of God:

> When he entered on his ministry in Simprin there
> was not a single house in which family worship was
> observed: within a period of less than seven years there
> was not a single home in all the parish without its family
> altar and its morning and evening sacrifice of praise and
> prayer. As it had been with Baxter at Kidderminster,
> when at the stated hours every house resounded with
> the voice of psalms, so it had come to be the experience
> of Boston in the cottages of this rural parish.[8]

Little wonder that he could write at the end of it all, 'I parted
with a people whose hearts were knit to me, and mine to them.'
It was 'the sense of God's command' that alone constrained him
to leave.[9]

What a different place was Ettrick! It had been without a
minister for four years and had become a moral and spiritual
wilderness. His biographer writes,

> At the first ... and for some time after, he was
> greatly shocked and discouraged by the indecent

and disorderly behaviour of many of the people
during divine worship, some of them rising with
rude noise and seeming impatience, and others
who had never entered the church, walking up and
down in the surrounding churchyard with loud
talking while the service was proceeding.[10]

Those who did sit through the services, for the most part, paid
little attention. Serious sin was also prevalent, especially 'profane
swearing, even among those who frequented public ordinances'
and 'sins of impurity, even in their grosser forms'.[11]

We are not surprised to learn that 'nothing ... but the sense of
the divine call to this new sphere and his faith in Him who could
"make his strength equal to his day", could have kept him from
fearing and even fainting at the prospect which opened before
him'.[12]

THOMAS CHALMERS

In contrast to both Dickie and Boston, Thomas Chalmers,
in his Glasgow charge, had both an adequate building and
crowds of people who hung breathlessly on his lips. But he had
his difficulties too, in his case, a mass of extra-congregational
activities. He may have been assured on the point before going
to Glasgow (as suggested in the quotation near the beginning of
this chapter), but the reality—at least in the early days—meant
a hard fight for him. Writing of the 'peculiarities' of Glasgow's
citizens, he says,

> The peculiarity which bears hardest upon me is the
> incessant demand they have, upon all occasions, for the
> personal attendance of the ministers. They must have
> four to every funeral or they do not think it has been
> genteelly gone through; they must have one or more to
> all the committees of the societies; they must fall in at
> every procession ... I gave in to all this at first, but I am
> beginning to keep a suspicious eye upon these repeated

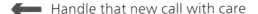

demands ever since I sat nearly an hour in grave
deliberation with a number of others upon a subject
connected with the property of a corporation, and that
subject was a *gutter*, and the question was whether it
should be bought and covered up, or let alone and left
to lie open. I am gradually separating myself from all
this trash, and long to establish it as a doctrine, that
the life of a town minister should be what the life of a
country minister might be; ... his entire time disposable
to the purposes to which the apostles gave themselves
wholly—that is the ministry of the Word and prayer.'[13]

A change meant *difficulties* for these men. For the first it was
the building, for the second, the people, for the third, the
expectations and duties that distracted him from the work of
the ministry. And in Dickie's case the problem was so severe
that it led to depression and other serious health concerns.

Examples like this can easily be paralleled—and multiplied.
With modern amplification systems acoustically poor buildings
need no longer be a hindrance to hearing. But what pastor is
not aware of the countless other problems that can arise over a
building! The size of the debt, the cost of repairs, the inadequacy
of the heating system, the problems associated with the age of the
property, the frustration of not being able to afford to purchase
or replace a building, differing opinions (often strongly held)
on how to address the issues; the new pastor may find himself
burdened with one or more of them.

And then there are the people. An older minister who
befriended me when I was a divinity student used to say to
me often, 'Where you have people, you have problems.' The
minister who leaves one congregation for another simply
exchanges one set of people-problems for another. And in his
new congregation these may be more numerous, more severe,

more intractable, more painful than any he has experienced before—some of them, perhaps, only coming to light after his settlement. There may be opposition to his preaching, resistance to change, people taking umbrage and leaving the congregation, a former pastor whose influence is unhelpful, a lack of support from certain elders; the list could go on and on.

Or take Chalmers' problem. A minister today may not find himself in grave discussion over gutters (or over what soup to serve to the inmates of the town hospital, either pork broth or broth of oxhead: an even more ludicrous discussion in which Chalmers found himself![14]). There may, however, be all kinds of expectations which, if yielded to, will make serious inroads into the time he should be devoting to the work of the ministry; expectations which it will be no small task for him to be relieved of.

And the *effect* of these difficulties? We saw how seriously they affected Matthew Dickie. The impact on the new pastor today may be just as major. Depression, other health issues, anger, bitterness, frustration, misgivings as to the wisdom of accepting the call, the fear that a mistake has been made, the futile wish that one could turn the clock back, the temptation to resign; these are all things that ministers have had to wrestle with on account of the difficulties associated with the change.

A biblical perspective
It is instructive in the light of these difficulties to think about Paul and his experiences in Philippi. After delivering the slave girl from the spirit that had possessed her, he and Silas were dragged into the market place, falsely accused, severely flogged, thrown into prison and there put in the stocks. Had he made a mistake in going to Philippi? There is not the least evidence to suggest that he had. It was the clear call of God that took him to Macedonia in the first place, and Philippi was the natural place to begin. Following God's leading *led* to difficulties for Paul in

Philippi—as it did elsewhere in Macedonia. So it does for God's servants today. It is no proof that we have mistaken the call of God when we find ourselves facing serious problems in a new situation. It is instead part of the course.

Following God's leading, however, led to more than difficulties for Paul. It also led to great blessing. Much came of this Macedonian mission. There were *converts*: Lydia, the jailer, the jailer's family, converts in Thessalonica, in Berea, in Athens, and in Corinth. *Churches* were established in Philippi, Thessalonica and Corinth. *Inspired letters* were written to these churches and later incorporated, along with Luke's *inspired history* of the mission, in our New Testament Scriptures. These New Testaments have in turn been launched upon the *world*. And as the letters and the history have been read and preached, incalculable blessing has come to multitudes! Isn't it thrilling?

God's blessing

Pastors who at God's bidding take up another charge may reckon upon the same two experiences. There will certainly be difficulties—some of them foreseen, others of them unforeseen. But there will certainly also be blessing. God sends us to places and people that we might be the means in his hand of doing *good*. And good will be done, notwithstanding the problems. Our labour in the Lord will not be in vain.

In 1622, the Revd Robert Bruce was exiled for a second time to Inverness in the north-east of Scotland. He was almost seventy years of age. On the day of his departure he was seen to pause before mounting his horse, and, for about a quarter of an hour, to stand with his eyes to heaven in silent meditation. A close friend, observing this, asked him about it. 'I was receiving my commission from my Master to go to Inverness,' was his reply, 'and He gave it me Himself, before I set my foot in the stirrup, and thither I go to sow a seed in Inverness that shall not be rooted out for many ages.'[15] And so it proved.

When it comes to the blessing that will rest upon *our* labours, we who are ministers will, for the most part, want to speak a great deal more tentatively. James Stalker, for example, said wisely,

> I do not pitch my expectations in the same high key
> as some of those who have called me; for I know
> how weak are my powers in comparison with the
> work needing to be done. But a step like this has
> to be taken in faith, and one must be content with
> such success as it may please God to give.[16]

In his case it proved to be considerable:

> St. Brycedale, Kirkcaldy, had always been notable for
> its loyalty to the evangel. During Stalker's ministry it
> stood out in more marked pre-eminence. The dynamic
> of the preacher, the elevation of his message, and the
> magnetism of his personality were realized by the
> whole community ... But it was in St. Matthew's,
> Glasgow, that he put on his strength. Every visitor
> to the thronged building with its massed ranks of
> worshippers felt the pulsing power of the preacher.
> A visitor declared that the most uplifting service
> he had ever attended was that of the celebration
> of the Lord's Supper in St. Matthew's—a service,
> he affirmed, which would convince any scornful
> unbeliever of the real presence of the Lord.[17]

One wonders, however, if there has ever been greater blessing upon a new ministry than that which rested upon C. H. Spurgeon's when, in 1854, he left the Cambridgeshire village of Waterbeach for New Park Street Chapel in London. For some years the congregation had been dwindling until in 1854 there were only around 200 in a building that could seat 1200. Under Spurgeon's ministry, however, it was soon crammed to the doors, eventually necessitating the building of the Metropolitan Tabernacle. In both buildings God worked in the most remarkable ways. Sinners were saved in great numbers. And through Spurgeon's published sermons (one a week for over sixty years) that saving work continues to this day all over the world.

It seems a far cry, of course, from the thousands gathering every Lord's Day to sit under Spurgeon's ministry to the comparative handfuls of people who make up so many of today's evangelical congregations—at least in the UK. But if the ministers who are over these congregations are there because the Head of the church has placed them there, they may look expectantly to that Head for his blessing. The 'quantity' may not seem all that great. Perhaps as the years go by it may even seem to diminish. But there is far more happening than meets the eye. Much more comes of a faithful ministry than it is possible to estimate. Let any man in a new charge, therefore, who is discouraged because of the difficulties, labour on in his Master's strength. He will not do so in vain.

ENDNOTES

Introduction

1   Hezekiah Harvey, *The Pastor: His Qualifications and Duties* (New York: Backus, 1982), pp. 120–124.

2   Thomas K. Ascol, (ed.), *Dear Timothy: Letters on Pastoral Ministry* (Cape Coral, FL: Founders Press, 2004), pp. 359–375.

Chapter 1

1   Simon J. Kistemaker, *New Testament Commentary: Acts* (Grand Rapids, MI: Baker, 1990), p. 223.

2   Charles Hodge, *A Commentary on the Epistle to the Ephesians* (Grand Rapids, MI: Baker, 1980), p. 166.

3   Harvey, *The Pastor*, p. 124.

4   James M. Gordon, *James Denney (1856–1917): An Intellectual and Contextual Biography* (Eugene, OR: Wipf and Stock, 2006), p. 133.

5   Donald Fraser, *Thomas Chalmers, D.D., LL.D.* (London: Hodder and Stoughton, 1881), p. 59.

6   Harvey, *The Pastor*, p. 124.

7   James Stalker, *The Preacher and His Models* (London: Hodder and Stoughton, 1891), p. 17.

8   Ibid. pp. 18–19.

9   Quoted in Hamilton M. MacGill, *The Life of Hugh Heugh, D.D.* (Edinburgh: Johnstone and Hunter, 1852), p. 164.

10 William Hanna, *Memoirs of Dr. Chalmers,* vol. i (Edinburgh: Thomas Constable, 1850–1854), p. 447.

Chapter 2

1   Mrs. M. Main, *Memorials of the Life and Ministry of Thomas Main, D.D.* (Edinburgh: MacNiven and Wallace, 1883), p. 76.

2   Iain H. Murray, (ed.), *Diary of Kenneth*

A. MacRae (Edinburgh: Banner of Truth, 1980), p. 225.

3   MacGill, *The Life of Hugh Heugh*, p. 152.

4   Andrew Thomson, *Thomas Boston of Ettrick: His Life and Times* (London: T. Nelson and Sons, 1895), p. 89.

5   Dr B. M. Palmer, *The Life and Letters of James Henley Thornwell* (Edinburgh: Banner of Truth, 1974), p. 268.

Chapter 3

1   Derek Prime, *When Should a Minister Leave a Church?* Address given at the Westminster Fellowship [n.d.].

2   John Thornbury, *A Pastor in New York: The Life and Times of Spencer Cone* (Darlington: Evangelical Press, 2004), p. 71.

3   Main, *Memorials*, p. 72.

4   F. W. Boreham, *My Pilgrimage* (London: Epworth Press, 1954), p. 177.

5   Thornbury, *A Pastor in New York*, p. 72.

6   Mrs. A. Fleming, *Autobiography of the Rev. William Arnot and Memoir* (London: James Nisbet & Co., 1877), p. 387.

7   Quoted in ibid. p. 391.

8   W. M. Taylor, *Memoir of the Rev. Matthew Dickie* (Bristol: W. Mack, [n.d.]), p. 70.

9   Main, *Memorials*, p. 74.

10 MacGill, *The Life of Hugh Heugh*, p. 166.

11 Boreham, *My Pilgrimage*, p. 206.

12 Ibid. p. 217.

13 Ibid. pp. 178–179.

14 Palmer, *The Life and Letters*, pp. 265–266.

15 Thomson, *Thomas Boston of Ettrick*, p. 90.

16 MacGill, *The Life of Hugh Heugh*, pp. 152–153.

17 Hanna, *Memoirs*, vol. iv, p. 311.

Chapter 4

1 Harvey, *The Pastor*, p. 120.

2 Ibid.

3 John Knox, *The History of the Reformation in Scotland* (London: A & C Black, 1899), p. 131.

4 Main, *Memorials*, p. 71.

5 Harvey, *The Pastor*, p. 120.

6 Ibid. p. 122.

7 Walter J. Chantry, email correspondence, 22 February 2008.

8 Fleming, Autobiography, p. 385.

9 Thomas Boston, *Memoirs of Thomas Boston* (Edinburgh: Banner of Truth, 1988), p. 192.

10 Ibid. p. 196.

11 Ibid.

12 Stalker, *The Preacher and His Models*, pp. 57–58.

Chapter 5

1 Boreham, *My Pilgrimage*, p. 176.

2 Harvey, *The Pastor*, p. 123.

3 Main, *Memorials*, p. 82.

4 Harvey, *The Pastor*, p. 123.

5 Murray, *Diary*, p. 145.

6 Ibid. p. 221.

7 Prime, *When Should a Minister Leave?*, p. 6.

8 Main, *Memorials*, p. 74.

9 Ibid. p. 85.

10 Murray, *Diary*, p. 147.

11 Ibid. p. 146.

12 Thomson, *Thomas Boston of Ettrick*, pp. 89–90.

13 Boreham, *My Pilgrimage*, p. 216.

14 Murray, *Diary*, p. 226.

15 P. K. Livingstone, *St Brycedale Church, Kirkcaldy: The Origin and History of St Brycedale Church* (Kirkcaldy: The Allen Lithographic Company Limited, 1957), p. 48.

16 Harvey, *The Pastor*, p. 123.

17 Alexander Stewart, *The Tree of Promise* (Edinburgh: William P. Kennedy, 1864), p. lii.

Chapter 6

1 Boreham, *My Pilgrimage*, p. 206.

2 Hanna, *Memoirs*, vol. i, p. 447.

3 Iain D. Campbell, email correspondence, 10 November 2008.

4 John Piper, *A Hunger for God* (Wheaton: IL: Crossway, 1997), p. 107.

5 Livingstone, *St Brycedale Church*, p. 47.

6 Fleming, *Autobiography*, p. 384.

7 Prime, *When Should a Minister Leave?*, p. 7.

8 MacGill, *The Life of Hugh Heugh*, p. 44.

9 Ibid. p. 152.

10 Ibid. p. 153.

11 Ibid. p. 155.

12 Ibid. p. 169.

13 Elizabeth King, *Memoir of the Rev. David King, LL.D.* (Glasgow: James Maclehose and Sons, 1885), p. 42.

14 William Steven and John Edmond, *Posthumous Discourses of the late Rev. James Stark, D.D. with an Introductory Memoir* (Edinburgh: A. Fullarton & Co., 1852), p. xc.

15 Iver Martin, email correspondence, 6 October 2008.

16 Ibid.

17 James Taylor, *Pastors Under Pressure* (Leominster: Day One, 2004), p. 81.

18 Boreham, *My Pilgrimage*, p. 178.

19 Palmer, *The Life and Letters*, pp. 276–277.

20 Boreham, *My Pilgrimage*, pp. 178–179.

Chapter 7

1 Murray, *Diary*, p. 147.

2 Hanna, *Memoirs*, vol. i, p. 454.

3 Ibid. pp. 454–455.

4 Adam Forman, *The Common Salvation and Other Discourses* (London: James Nisbet & Co., 1866), p. xv.

5 Livingstone, *St Brycedale Church*, p. 47.

6 Boreham, *My Pilgrimage*, p. 183.

7 Taylor, *Memoir*, pp. 80–81.

8 Thomson, *Thomas Boston of Ettrick*, p. 85.

9 Ibid. p. 92.

10 Ibid. p. 99.

11 Ibid. p. 100.

12 Ibid. p. 98.

13 Norman L. Walker, *Thomas Chalmers: His Life and Its Lessons* (London: T. Nelson and Sons, 1880), p. 53.

14 Ibid. p. 53.

15 D. C. MacNicol, *Robert Bruce* (London: Banner of Truth, 1961), p. 155.

16 Livingstone, *St Brycedale Church*, p. 48.

17 W. M. Clow, 'Obituary: The Rev. Professor Stalker, D.D.', in *The British Weekly*, [n.d.] February 1927.

FOR FURTHER HELP AND INFORMATION

Thomas K. Ascol, (ed.)., *Dear Timothy: Letters on Pastoral Ministry* (Cape Coral, FL: Founders Press, 2004).

Horatius Bonar, *Life of the Rev. John Milne, M.A.* (London: James Nisbet & Co., 1869)., Chs. 11 and 12.

F. W. Boreham, *My Pilgrimage* (London: Epworth Press, 1954).

Thomas Boston, *Memoirs of Thomas Boston* (Edinburgh: Banner of Truth, 1988).

Mrs. A. Fleming, *Autobiography of the Rev. William Arnot and Memoir* (London: James Nisbet & Co., 1877).

Adam Forman, *The Common Salvation and Other Discourses* (London: James Nisbet & Co., 1866).

Donald Fraser, *Thomas Chalmers, D.D., LL.D.* (London: Hodder and Stoughton, 1881).

James M. Gordon, *James Denney (1856–1917).: An Intellectual and Contextual Biography* (Eugene, OR: Wipf and Stock, 2006).

William Hanna, *Memoirs of Dr. Chalmers*, vols. i–iv (Edinburgh: Thomas Constable, 1850–1854).

Hezekiah Harvey, *The Pastor: His Qualifications and Duties* (New York: Backus, 1982).

Elizabeth King, *Memoir of the Rev. David King, LL.D.* (Glasgow: James Maclehose and Sons, 1885).

John Knox, *The History of the Reformation in Scotland* (London: A & C Black, 1899).

P. K. Livingstone, *St Brycedale Church, Kirkcaldy: The Origin and History of St Brycedale Church* (Kirkcaldy: The Allen Lithographic Company Limited, 1957).

Hamilton M. MacGill, *The Life of Hugh Heugh, D.D.* (Edinburgh: Johnstone and Hunter, 1852).

D. C. MacNicol, *Robert Bruce* (London: Banner of Truth, 1961).

Mrs. M. Main, *Memorials of the Life and Ministry of Thomas Main, D.D.* (Edinburgh: MacNiven and Wallace, 1883).

Iain H. Murray, (ed.)., *Diary of Kenneth A. MacRae* (Edinburgh: Banner of Truth, 1980).

Dr B. M. Palmer, *The Life and Letters of James Henley Thornwell* (Edinburgh: Banner of Truth, 1974).

John Piper, *A Hunger for God* (Wheaton: IL: Crossway, 1997).

James Stalker, *The Preacher and His Models* (London: Hodder and Stoughton, 1891).

William Steven and John Edmond, *Posthumous Discourses of the late Rev. James Stark, D.D. with an Introductory Memoir* (Edinburgh: A. Fullarton & Co., 1852).

Alexander Stewart, *The Tree of Promise* (Edinburgh: William P. Kennedy, 1864).

James Taylor, *Pastors Under Pressure* (Leominster: Day One, 2004).

W. M. Taylor, *Memoir of the Rev. Matthew Dickie* (Bristol: W. Mack, [n.d.]).

Andrew Thomson, *Thomas Boston of Ettrick: His Life and Times* (London: T. Nelson and Sons, 1895).

John Thornbury, *A Pastor in New York: The Life and Times of Spencer Cone* (Darlington: Evangelical Press, 2004).

Norman L. Walker, *Thomas Chalmers: His Life and Its Lessons* (London: T. Nelson and Sons, 180).

About Day One:

Day One's threefold commitment:
- To be faithful to the Bible, God's inerrant, infallible Word;
- To be relevant to our modern generation;
- To be excellent in our publication standards.

I continue to be thankful for the publications of Day One. They are biblical; they have sound theology; and they are relevant to the issues at hand. The material is condensed and manageable while, at the same time, being complete—a challenging balance to find. We are happy in our ministry to make use of these excellent publications.

JOHN MACARTHUR, PASTOR-TEACHER, GRACE COMMUNITY CHURCH, CALIFORNIA

It is a great encouragement to see Day One making such excellent progress. Their publications are always biblical, accessible and attractively produced, with no compromise on quality. Long may their progress continue and increase!

JOHN BLANCHARD, AUTHOR, EVANGELIST AND APOLOGIST

Visit our web site for more information and to request a free catalogue of our books.

www.dayone.co.uk

U.S. web site:

www.dayonebookstore.com

Also available

Make your church's money work
Achieving financial integrity in your congregation

JOHN TEMPLE

96PP, PAPERBACK

ISBN 978-1-84625-150-4

The church's finances are a real concrete expression of its vision, its priorities and its commitment to doing things 'decently and in order'. This book examines the basis of sound biblical stewardship as applied to the practical aspects of budgeting, reporting and control of expenses in a church. It suggests a remuneration policy for pastors and other paid workers and outlines the responsibilities of members in supporting their church. Examples of a spreadsheet for budgeting and reporting are included. It is written in non-accounting terminology and should be read by all leaders and anyone who spends any of the church's money.

'John Temple's book—often provocative, sometimes controversial—uses biblical principles, personal examples and a healthy dose of common sense, as well as giving many practical examples of how church finances could be managed. Few treasurers and leadership teams will fail to benefit from a careful consideration of the principles set out here.'

GARY BENFOLD, PASTOR, MOORDOWN BAPTIST CHURCH, BOURNEMOUTH, ENGLAND

'Make Your Church's Money Work is comprehensive but concise, and easy to read, understand and execute by clergy and laity alike. Its biblical foundation ensures its value and the personal illustrations demonstrate its practicality as a blueprint for fidelity to God and his gospel.'

DR REGGIE WEEMS, SENIOR PASTOR, HERITAGE BAPTIST CHURCH, JOHNSON CITY, TENNESSEE, USA

Also available

Comfort those who grieve
Ministering God's grace in times of loss

PAUL TAUTGES

144PP, PAPERBACK

ISBN 978-1-84625-155-9

Until the end of time, when the curse of sin is finally removed, suffering will be a large part of the human experience—and a large part of that suffering will be walking through the painful reality of death. Death is not foreign territory that ministers of grace walk upon. As a result, "Death," writes Paul Tautges, "provides a natural opportunity not only for ministry to others, but also for personal growth in ministers." Therefore, church shepherds must not waste these precious and painful occasions that God provides for the demonstration of mercy and the advantage of the gospel.

This book is a treasure chest of pastoral theology that will equip ministers to reach out to those who grieve with the Christ-centered comfort of God rooted in the gospel. The theological foundation espoused here, as well as the numerous practical helps that are included, will help any servant of the Lord to point the hearts and minds of the bereaved to the "man of sorrows" who is "acquainted with grief" (Isa. 53:3).

'Every minister of the gospel will find this book helpful. We are given concrete ideas for consoling those who are dying and then on preparing funeral messages which not only comfort the grieving, but also challenge the lost with a clear gospel message. I know of no book like *Comfort Those Who Grieve*. Most "how to" books are shallow and often devoid of deep theological content. This excellent book is an exception.'

CURTIS C. THOMAS, PASTOR FOR OVER FIFTY YEARS, BIBLE TEACHER, AND AUTHOR OF LIFE IN THE BODY

'Here is biblical, insightful, and practical advice regarding serving those who grieve. Written with the tenderness and understanding of a gentle pastor, this book will be a helpful manual for those who guide others through the valley of the shadow of death. I hope it gains wide distribution!'

DR. LES LOFQUIST, IFCA INTERNATIONAL EXECUTIVE DIRECTOR

Also available

Discipline with care
Applying biblical correction in your church

STEPHEN MCQUOID

96PP, PAPERBACK

ISBN 978-1-84625-152-8

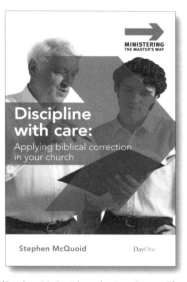

Discipline is one of the most difficult issues in contemporary church life. Church leaders often need to battle to maintain the integrity of their churches, sometimes with tragic results. But why is it so hard? Should we bother with it at all?

In this thorough treatment of the subject, Stephen McQuoid answers these questions and provides a biblical framework for church discipline. Because prevention is better than cure, he shows that discipline is not just about punishing but includes a whole way of life which keeps us spiritually accountable and in a right relationship with God. Corrective discipline will also at times be necessary, and he guides us through the disciplinary stages taught in the New Testament. By using appropriate case studies, he also demonstrates the complications of real-life situations and highlights the lessons that can be learned.

'Stephen McQuoid emphasises the need for leaders not to shirk the correction of members no matter how difficult. In exercising discipline the church is giving God's verdict on the given situation. There must, therefore, be both judgement and compassion. Helpful advice is given to both leaders and members as to what kind of attitude should be displayed towards the offender.'

DAVID CLARKSON, ELDER AT CARTSBRIDGE EVANGELICAL CHURCH AND AUTHOR OF 'LEARNING TO LEAD' COURSE

'In any local church, the issues of authority, discipline and leadership lie close to the surface. Stephen's book explores succinctly some of the cultural issues, scriptural context and practical outworkings of the vital need to keep the body in shape.'

ANDREW LACEY, CHURCH ELDER, MANAGER GLO BOOK SHOP, DIRECTOR OF PARTNERSHIP, SCOTLAND

Also available

Visit the sick
Shepherding the afflicted and dying in your congregation

BRIAN CROFT

96PP, PAPERBACK

ISBN 978-1-84625-143-6

The demands of the twenty-first-century have led to the neglect of certain essential responsibilities in the life of a Christian. One of those is the visitation and care of the sick in our congregations. This book is designed to instruct and motivate pastors, church leaders, and other care-giving Christians through the counsel of our heroes of church history, to recapture the practice of visiting the sick. This is accomplished by considering three specific areas. First, is our commitment to the theological as we consider how to most effectively care for their souls. Second, is our commitment to the pastoral, which instructs us how to proceed with wisdom and discernment in the variety of circumstances we will face. Third, is our commitment to the practical so that the manner in which we care for the sick will help, not hinder our effort to communicate biblical truth to them.

'Many younger pastors (and not so young ones as well) have never received the sort of very practical guidance which Brian Croft gives in this book. It will now be a recommended text in my Pastoral Ministries class.'

RAY VAN NESTE, PH.D., ASSOCIATE PROFESSOR OF CHRISTIAN STUDIES, DIRECTOR, R. C. RYAN CENTER FOR BIBLICAL STUDIES, UNION UNIVERSITY, ELDER, CORNERSTONE COMMUNITY CHURCH

'Church member, let this book equip you to become more useful to those in your church who are ailing. Young pastor, gain from Brian's practical wisdom. Seasoned pastor, let this book remind you of the privilege it is to serve and encourage the sick in a fallen world. I plan to read it together with our elders, and hope to make it available to our congregation as an equipping tool.'

PAUL ALEXANDER, SENIOR PASTOR, FOX VALLEY BIBLE CHURCH, ST. CHARLES, IL, CO-AUTHOR, THE DELIBERATE CHURCH

Also available

Look after your voice
Taking care of the preacher's greatest asset

MIKE MELLOR

96PP, PAPERBACK

ISBN 978-1-84625-125-2

As a hammer is to a carpenter, a scalpel to a surgeon, a trowel to a brick mason or a needle to a tailor—so the voice is to a preacher. Man's voice is the primary means God uses to deliver His Word to mankind, yet how often we who are called to impart the most important truths in the world are apt to neglect, if not wilfully abuse our all-vital 'tool of the trade'. Can there be any more pitiful sight in all nature than a God-sent preacher who is forced to be silent? We are not thinking here however of a silence brought about by pressure from ungodly sources, but that which has been enforced because of the preacher's own negligence concerning his voice. Mike Mellor's goal is not to produce another speech book (of which a good number can be found, usually aimed at actors or singers) but that something of our high calling as God's spokesmen may be re-kindled and as a consequence our desire to care for the frail vehicle God has designed to convey his Word may be increased.

'… I haven't seen anything like it for years, so it fits a good and helpful niche in the market … If, like me, you are prepared to pay the social cost of conditioning your voice by compulsive 'humming', you should still buy this little volume for the serious advice it contains.'

JONATHAN STEPHEN, PRINCIPAL, WALES EVANGELICAL SCHOOL OF THEOLOGY AND DIRECTOR, AFFINITY

'In much of our modern preaching, a great deal of catching up is necessary in terms of actual effective delivery. This book by an open-air preacher will help us in our public speaking—even if our voices never have quite the resonance of a John Chrysostom, a Whitefield or a Billy Graham. I certainly intend to put into prayerful practice the invaluable suggestions and exercises given us by Mike Mellor.'

RICO TICE, CO-AUTHOR OF *CHRISTIANITY EXPLORED* AND ASSOCIATE MINISTER AT ALL SOULS CHURCH, LONDON

Also available

Counsel your flock
Fulfilling your role as a teaching shepherd

PAUL TAUTGES

96PP, PAPERBACK

ISBN 978-1-84625-154-2

The ministry of counseling has for too long been relegated to the professional counselor. Paul Tautges brings the biblical command for discipleship right back to the local church and to all believers. Rather than send people who are struggling spiritually, socially, and emotionally to a limited group of professionals, Tautges makes the case theologically that the responsibility for all church members is to disciple one another and to restore hurting people.

In this companion to his previous book, *Counsel One Another*, he makes it clear that for this one-another ministry to take place it is essential that pastors understand the key role that they play in the discipleship process. Believers need a way to measure their pastor's discipleship philosophy and skills and pastors need a way to teach them to be involved in the counseling, discipleship, restoring-one-another ministry.

'This book gets it right! Comprehensive and convincing, *Counsel Your Flock* shows how true biblical counseling and preaching fit hand-in-glove. Those who preach, teach, or counsel regularly are sure to benefit greatly from this helpful resource.'

DR. JOHN MACARTHUR, PASTOR-TEACHER OF GRACE COMMUNITY CHURCH IN SUN VALLEY, CALIFORNIA

'The ministry of counseling has for too long been relegated to the professional counselor. Paul Tautges brings the biblical command for discipleship right back to the local church and to all believers.

This is a book about local church discipleship, of which leadership is a big part. *Counsel Your Flock* addresses an important need. This is a must read!'

DR. RON ALLCHIN, EXECUTIVE DIRECTOR OF THE BIBLICAL COUNSELING CENTER IN ARLINGTON HEIGHTS, ILLINOIS